THE UNDERERS

By

Justin Christopher

For Amy

CHAPTER 1

If you asked Journee Blake what she most wanted in this world, the answer would be to have her very own bedroom. Oh, to have her own space, one she could decorate with her favourite posters and artwork, where she could play her ukulele as loud as she wanted. Or try on new clothes without her brother farting in her face. Oh, to have her own mirror, her very own desk on which to do her homework, and no stinky Power Rangers undies lying on the floor.

But that was the problem. Journee and her younger brother Miles had shared the same room since they were both toddlers.

In her mind, Miles was without doubt, the

most annoying brother in the world. Apart from his obvious gas problems, and his love of hiding Journee's belongings, and saying things like 'I hate you,' and 'I wish you'd die,' and 'Nobody loves you,' he also thought it was hilarious to place spiders beneath his sister's pillow just before lights-out.

Journee wasn't a scaredy cat, not by any means, but one thing she could not tolerate was the sight of spiders. Even when Miles couldn't find one, he would creep up to Journee and pretend he had one in his clenched fist.

Aren't brothers just hilarious?

Journee Blake would be the first to admit that she had a less than normal childhood. Most normal children aren't made to attend seven different schools before their tenth birthday.

Just imagine that for a minute. Seven NEW schools! That's seven times you had to make new friends. Seven different school uniforms. Seven new teachers. Can you imagine!

Now don't go thinking Journee Blake was a bad student, because she was actually very bright. The problem was her father, Bill Blake. More to the point, the problem was Bill Blake's job. He was a policeman. A very bad one.

How bad? Well, once he locked himself in jail while eleven blind robbers escaped. Another time he broke into City Hall at midnight because he needed to pee. And who could ever forget Constable Blake's infamous school talk where he put handcuffs on the teacher as a joke and forgot where he put the keys?

Bill Blake lost seven jobs in seven years and each time he did Journee was forced to leave what friends she had, and drive hundreds of miles across the country.

Each time the Blake family moved into a new house Journee spent the first few months feeling very sad, and very sorry for herself. Mostly because everything was different. The house smelt different. It felt different. Nothing was where it was supposed to be. She could no longer walk down the hallway with her eyes closed. Her new bedroom had once belonged to someone else. We're talking someone else's germs. Someone else's breath. Their arguments. Their toenails. Their worries, and their dirty old socks behind the heater.

But after six months, and Journee always found it to be exactly six months, her house became a home. Gone were the worries and the toenails and the bad breath. Such nasty things were replaced with Journee's favourites – the smell of jasmine and honey, Nutella in the kitchen, and Bob Marley's reggae music playing loudly in her headphones.

Then Bill Blake would get fired again and Journee's world flipped upside down.

On a murky morning in the middle of June, the Blake family moved into their run-down house at number 88 Cabbage Tree Avenue in the town of Millwater.

This particular day, Journee and her brother Miles stood in the hallway as their father, an incredibly tall man with a chest that stuck out like a bathroom sink, muttered the words no child wants to hear.

'You two are sharing,' said Mr Blake. 'Huh? I don't want to share with her!' Miles snapped.

'But, Dad,' Journee pleaded. 'There are three rooms, remember? One for you and Mum. One for me and one for Miles. You promised when we moved again we'd have our own rooms! You promised!'

Her father winked at Journee. 'I know I did, honey,' he said. 'But where will Ringo and Moses sleep?'

Ringo and Moses were unfriendly old dogs, big snarly beasts with shark-like teeth. And even though these ugly mutts loved nothing better than biting holes in the trousers of unsuspecting children, Bill Blake treated them like princes. They always got the last scrap of food. They always got the front seat in the car. And now these slobbering brats had their own room.

Journee already hated this house. For a start, it was old and every single door jammed, or stuck, or creaked. It was a one-level bungalow with a cramped lounge, an even smaller kitchen, and a backyard only just big enough to house the family's four chickens.

There was also a very old house alarm on the wall by the front door. So old and so strange that Journee would never have guessed it was a house alarm at all. It looked more like someone from a hundred years ago had glued a rusty old shoebox to a wall. Unlike modern alarms, there were no flashing lights or electronic numbers on its interface. Instead, there was a single handle attached to the box, which pointed to

ON or OFF.

Right now Mr Blake was explaining in great detail how to use it, but even her father, who professed to knowing everything about everything, was struggling to speak.

He pulled Journee and Miles closer together as his chubby fingers hovered over the prehistoric piece of junk.

'Now, this,' he said, 'is quite a find. I have never in all my time in the police force seen one quite like it.' Journee could tell her father was impressed because as he talked he stroked the ancient alarm as if it were a baby panda.

Journee and Miles moved even closer to get a better look, trying their very best to appear impressed.

'Once we've settled in, I'll get us a new one,' said Mr Blake. 'I'll no doubt get a free one from the police station. I might even sell this one to the local museum. I bet it's worth a fortune. But for now, remember to switch it to ON when we leave the house, and switch it…' '-OFF!' said Miles.

'…when we come home. Correct, son!'

Miles poked his tongue out at his sister.

Journee's favourite time of day was breakfast, mostly because if she and her mum got up early enough, it was just the girls. Just her and her mama, Betty Blake, talking about the world over hot tea. As usual, Betty started making the meal, but Journee had to finish it, despite her cooking abilities being limited to one dish. Chocolate brownies were her speciality; she'd found a foolproof recipe which required both white and dark chocolate, and came out of the oven warm, chewy and squidgy. This morning's menu, however, was scrambled eggs with cream, with buttery toast on the side.

'Sorry about the new uniform,' said her mother, smiling. 'Not exactly fashionable.'

Journee sighed. 'It's not your fault, Mum. Um, I was wondering if maybe we could talk about my room? Because Dad said that when we moved I could have-' '-Eggs! Coffee! Let's go! Ringo, get that out of your mouth! Moses, do that again and I'll rub your nose in it!' Mr Bill Blake, fresh from his cold shower, entered the kitchen with his trousers pulled all the way up to his armpits. He looked at his plate and nodded approvingly. 'Where's my knife and fork?' he asked.

'What, no tomato SAUCE?'

As usual there was no 'please' or 'thank you.'

As Journee closed the cutlery drawer she heard a noise coming from the cupboard next to the stove. It was a scratching noise, a scuttling, scurrying, scampering noise.

She leapt back in a wild panic, the knife and fork landing inches from her bare feet.

'Did anyone else hear that!' she yelped. 'There's...what's in there?'

Mr Blake stood abruptly. 'Fine!' he said. 'I'll get my own sauce.'

Journee stared at the cupboard. The noises continued. They were slightly fainter now. What were they exactly? Rats? Insects? Ghosts?

She very quietly got a new knife and fork from the drawer. Miles slouched at the table, his long fingers dipped in his scrambled eggs.

Betty tidied her copious papers. 'Can I tell anyone about my new business idea?' she asked.

Journee's eyes hadn't left the cupboard. 'Um, yeah, of course, Mum.'

'You always say that,' she replied,

smiling. 'Thank you.'

'Well, one of these businesses has to work, doesn't it?' Journee replied.

'What are you saying?' Betty teased, scrolling to the correct page on her iPad. 'Okay, okay, here we go. And promise me you won't laugh.'

'We won't,' said Mr Blake, who was feeding the dogs scrambled eggs from his fork.

Betty looked up from her iPad. 'Karaoke, but it's *waterproof*! Waterproof karaoke!'

'Betty, seriously, outta all of your ideas-' Mr Blake started.

'-No, listen!' said Betty. 'Who doesn't love to sing in the shower? We all do, but who can ever remember the words? Waterproof karaoke! I need to register the domain name before anyone steals it, then I'll make some calls. This is going to make us rich. Someone feed the chickens!'

Mr Blake pulled his wife's plate over and put it onto the floor. Slurp went the dogs. 'So,' he said to the children. 'Know how to get to school?'

'Not really,' Journee replied.

'Down Millwater Ave,' Mr Blake replied. 'Left

at the lights. Straight ahead. Turn right. Past the roundabout. Gas station on right. School's straight ahead.'

'But, Dad, it's our first day,' Journee said. 'Do you think maybe you could drop us off?'

'It's raining,' said Miles.

Mr Blake gulped down his coffee and grabbed the dogs by their collars. 'Can't, sorry! Late, very late!' he said. 'It's my first day too, you know. I need to make a good impression!'

Journee always worried about the same things the day she started a new school. In no particular order, these worries were:

People staring.

People talking behind her back.

Forgetting people's names as soon as she heard them.

People saying her name wrong. People spelling her name wrong.

But there were two worries that worried Journee more than all of those worries combined. They were:

Her weight.

The way she breathed.

Journee knew she was bigger than most other kids, but it never stopped anyone telling her. As if that wasn't bad enough, she also had a habit of breathing loudly. Very loudly. A mean-spirited girl once told her the noise she made was like a waste disposal clogged with eggshells.

Her mother always told her the way she breathed wasn't her fault. A constant chest infection and a twisted bone in her nose were to blame. The doctor said there was nothing she could do.

Journee's new teacher was named Miss Carboni. Unlike other teachers at Millwater School, who chose to wear sensible clothes like track pants and cardigans, Miss Carboni wore eight-inch high-heeled shoes and tight leopard-skin pants.

Journee walked gingerly into Room 5 and found a spare desk. Other children seemed to ignore her.

This was a small miracle. No one called her fat, or said she breathed like Darth Vader.

Everything was going well. Too well. Miss Carboni clip-clopped her way about the classroom, her bangles and bracelets jingling and jangling. She dropped assignments on desks as she went. Children held their noses, her perfume almost singeing their nostrils.

'We start the year as we mean to go on!' said Miss Carboni. 'We work hard! No time for sleep! Or dreams! Or acting the clown!' She slapped a piece of paper in front of Journee. 'Understand?'

'Yes…Miss Carboni?'

Journee flipped her assignment over. It was English. She froze. She despised English. All those nouns, pronouns and adjectives! Who knew the difference?

More to the point, who cared?

Journee read the first question: *Explain in one paragraph the difference between a noun and a pronoun, giving an example of each.* She found herself chewing on a red pen. A few minutes later it exploded. Her hand was covered in red ink. The whole class ran outside.

'She's bitten her tongue off!' the children yelled. 'Ew, get away from me, FATTY VAMPIRE!'

Journee tried her best to tell everyone what had happened, that the so-called blood was actually ink, but all she could think of was trying not to swallow the bitter liquid.

The screams continued. Journee attempted to run to the bathroom, but the school nurse placed her into a wheelchair.

'Call an ambulance!' yelled the nurse.

It took Journee ages to explain to the nurse, Miss Carboni, and the school principal that the so-called blood was nothing more than red pen ink.

'Stay in sick bay regardless,' said the nurse. 'You're breathing funny.'

Journee Blake jumped into the back seat of her mum's car, hid beneath her hoodie and listened to Bob Marley.

Along with being the worst policeman in the world, Mr Blake was also the World's Worst Cook. You might disagree, of course. Maybe your father's egg fried rice once caught on fire, or your mother's watery lasagne was so bad even stray dogs wouldn't have touched it. But rest assured, as bad as those meals sound, compared to Mr Blake, your parents would be gourmet chefs. Tonight's menu was burnt lamb chops and cold Brussels sprouts.

Miles looked at his plate as if it were an overflowing toilet. Journee had to agree, as her own plate offered very few edible options. And boy, did Mr Blake notice.

'What's wrong?' he asked.

Miles could think of thousands of things.

However, if he named any of them he would have become dinner himself, so it was lucky for him that a familiar voice sounded seconds later.

'Hi, everyone!' said Betty, bursting through the front door with a handbag full of papers. 'Been working on waterproof karaoke. Soon this will be in showers all over the world!'

Journee smiled at her mum, who sat beside her and offered a loving squeeze. Journee sifted through her mum's notes, her mind on other things.

Seconds later, there was another scratching noise from the cupboard. The same scratching noise she had heard at breakfast. And – was that a voice?

Journee shuffled closer to her mum, who looked to Mr Blake. 'How was your first day at work, dear?' 'Buncha losers!' Mr Blake replied. 'Just like the last police department'.

Betty moved on just as Mr Blake shovelled a large spoonful of chops and sprouts into his mouth. 'What about you, Miles?' she asked.

'I didn't go to work,' Miles replied.

His mother sighed, punching her son lightly on the arm.

Miles put his fork down and cleared his throat. 'You want to know how my day was? Okay, then. My teacher Miss Moyle is SO dumb. She said I had FUR BALL diarrhoea! And I was like, what? How would she know I had FUR BALL diarrhoea? I don't even have diarrhoea! And if I did have diarrhoea, but I don't, it wouldn't have FUR BALLS in it! She is soooooooo dumb.'

'Were you talking too much?' Journee asked. 'What's that gotta do with it?' Miles asked. 'She probably said you had *verbal* diarrhoea,'

Journee replied. 'Which means you don't know when to keep your trap shut. I would say your teacher knows you pretty well already.'

'Shut up, Miss Know Everything!' said Miles.

'Tell us about your day.'

All eyes were on Journee, who folded her arms

and chewed. 'It was okay, I guess,' Journee said, quietly.

'Ask her about her new nickname,' cried Miles. 'Shut up,' Journee replied.

'You shut up, Fatty Vampire!'

'Shut! Up!' Journee repeated, and politely left the table. It took all of her energy to open her bedroom door, which seemed to be forever jammed shut.

Miles came in next, playing his video game at full volume. Journee put her headphones on and wondered if she would ever find a school where she wasn't teased.

Ringo and Moses weren't the only pets in the Blake household. Miles also had a little friend who lived in an old glass fish tank in a small room off the kitchen, which, as it happens, was the perfect home for a Chilean Rose Tarantula.

There were two reasons Miles loved Webster.

The boy absolutely loved spiders.

His sister absolutely *hated* them.

Most people would think such a creature would kill you in seconds, but Webster was actually very tame. He loved nothing more than walking across someone's bare feet. Miles longed for the day Journee brought a friend home so he could scare the living daylights out of them. But that never happened, so the boy would stare at his eight-legged friend and watch him eat live crickets and rummage about his home made of leaves and soil. Sometimes, just to get a reaction, he would prod him with a stick to see the spider rear up and expose his fangs.

Tonight there were no spiders, which didn't mean Miles wasn't living up to his title as World's Most Annoying Brother. As Journee lay on her bed she watched in disgust as the crazy boy taped red string between his bed and the desk in the middle of the room. He had divided the room in half and even had a sign which read 'STEP OVER THIS YOU DIIIIIEEEEEE!'

'So childish,' Journee muttered. 'You are,' replied Miles.

Journee put on her headphones and began writing a list in her diary. She called it 'Five ways I can get my own bedroom.' But apart from locking out Miles altogether, she couldn't think of a single idea. She threw the diary on the bed and turned the music up.

After their second day at school Journee and Miles trudged home in the driving rain. Puddles transformed into small lakes and gutters raged like streams. The children tried to use their bags as umbrellas, but the rain was too heavy. They shivered and shook like puppies in a drain. Half a block from home, Mr Blake pulled up beside them.

'Good timing!' said Mr Blake, speaking through a tiny gap in the window so as not to get wet.

Once home, Mr Blake unlocked the front door.

He yanked the arm of the old alarm into the OFF position, the force of which caused his forefinger and thumb to sting.

'Stupid old machine!' he cursed, and watched as Miles dragged his school bags down the hallway, leaving a soaked trail behind them. Journee's dripping sweater stuck to her body and her wet socks seemed to be glued to her legs.

Seconds later Mr Blake stood before them, his face the colour of beetroot. He marched the children into the lounge as if they were going to prison. Pens, paper and pillows covered the floor. It was an almighty mess. There were leftover cookie crumbs, empty chip packets, plastic bottles and dozens of books scattered across the couch.

'How many times have I told you to pick things up after yourselves?' asked Mr Blake.

'Don't look at me,' said Journee. 'They're not mine.'

'They're not mine either,' said Miles.

'So we have a messy ghost living here, then?' Mr Blake asked.

'I didn't do this!' said Journee. 'It was probably Miles.'

Miles said, 'She's just saying that so I get into trouble!'

Soon the doorbell rang. Mr Blake nursed his hand and opened the door in a huff.

'Hello, sir,' said the boy on the doorstep, who was wearing a dirty apron and an oversized cap. 'Four pepperoni pizzas?'

'Wrong house!' said Mr Blake, about to shut the door in the poor boy's face.

The delivery boy wedged the pizza boxes into

the closing gap. 'Ah, sir,' he stammered. '88 Cabbage Tree Avenue?'

'Yes,' replied Mr Blake. 'But we didn't order any pizzas.'

Mr Blake slammed the door and turned around to find Betty standing millimetres from his face.

'You made the bed this morning! Thank you,' she said, and kissed him on the cheek.

'I…did I? Ah, okay, then,' Mr Blake said, and walked down the hallway shaking his head.

That night as she tossed and turned, Journee was surprised to see Miles was also awake.

'By the way,' she said, 'I never said you could use my pens.'

'I never used your pens!' replied Miles.

'You used my pens and you made a mess in the lounge.'

'I told you a trillion times,' Miles replied. 'It wasn't me.'

'Who made the mess, then?' Journee asked.

Miles sighed and rolled over. 'Mum must have done some colouring-in.'

'Very funny,' Journee sighed. 'I don't like this

house.'

'Journee, you don't like any house.'

'This one's creepy,' she replied. 'I can feel things.'

There was a rustle of sheets. A gust of wind slapped the window.

'What…sort of things?' Miles asked a few minutes later. 'And please don't say ghosts.'

'Weird things,' Journee mumbled. 'There is something alive in this house. I can feel it. I know you don't believe me, but something is living here.'

There was silence.

'With us,' said Journee.

Early the next morning Journee opened the camera on her phone. A plan was brewing. An experiment. A way to prove to her father she wasn't lying about the mess. She took photos of the lounge, the bathroom and the kitchen. All three rooms were absolutely spotless, not so much as a cushion out of place. Her experiment was under way.

CHAPTER 2

A week passed and as usual Miles made friends with most of the school. For some reason other kids thought he was cool and funny and popular. This was a mystery to Journee who knew her brother to be obnoxious, annoying, smelly and dumb.

She comforted herself by thinking about the thousands of friends she made when she was as young as Miles. It was so much easier it was to make friends back then. But she stopped herself. It wasn't easier at all. Who would want a sleepover with a Fatty Vampire?

Today Miss Carboni asked a volunteer to feed Pumpkin and Goldilocks, Room 5's two goldfish. This should have been fun, right? But not to Journee. You see, doing something, anything in front of a classroom full of beady-eyed strangers was about the worst thing that could happen.

Journee took a deep breath and walked towards the tank. They're just two hungry little fish, she told herself, that's all. *Just feed the wee fish*. But the packet seemed to be glued shut. After twisting and yanking it, Journee decided to bite it, but when she did the packet flew apart like a piñata at a child's birthday party.

Fish food flew over the teacher. And over the front row of the class.

And all over Journee's sweaty face.

'Duh! You're supposed to tear it open from the other end!'

'Here's a clue. That's not the way you do it!' 'She's not Fatty, she's Fishy Vampire!'

The fish food clouded the water giving it the appearance of an underwater sandstorm. Miss Carboni scooped the two fish out so they wouldn't die during maths. Bonnie-Kate, the shortest girl in class, who Journee hadn't noticed before, picked the food up from the floor.

She looked up and smiled. 'Don't worry,' she said. 'We've got those bags at home. They're the worst things to open.'

At lunch no one sat next to Journee.

Making friends had gotten no easier since moving to Millwater.

————

As usual, Miles didn't stop for breath once on the drive home from school. As well as talking complete and utter nonsense, he also snuck into the front seat and ate the last peppermint from the glove compartment. Which should have stopped him from talking, but the sugar obviously turned him into a motor-mouth. The more he talked, and the more questions he asked, the larger the frown became on Betty's forehead.

'So why can't I stay at Hugo's house?' he asked. 'Because you went to bed late last night,' replied

Betty. 'And his brother drinks beer.' 'He's nineteen!' said Miles. 'The answer's no,' Betty replied.

'Dad smokes,' said Miles. 'And drinks beer.'

Betty whipped the keys out of the ignition and adjusted her hair in the rear-vision mirror. 'Your father's an adult,' she said.

Miles wasn't done. 'Dad said he started

smoking when he was nine.'

'Things were different then,' said Betty.

'So you were allowed to smoke when you were nine back, then?'

'Well, no, not everyone.'

'Just Dad? Because he was a policeman and he was allowed to?'

'Look, Miles, I'm not going to-'
'ARRRGGGHHHH!' screamed Journee, as the car swung into the driveway at 88 Cabbage Tree Avenue.

'OMG! OMG! OMG!'

There was something in the lounge. Something, Journee was sure of it. It walked from one side of the room to the other. It was dark grey in colour, its movements slow, like an old wooden doll. The thing, whatever it was, drew the curtains when it saw her.

'Mum, is our alarm on?' Journee asked. 'In the house?'

'Yes, dear, of course,' her mother replied. 'And please don't yell.'

Journee shook her head. 'No, it can't be,' she said. 'The alarm can't be on. I just saw someone in our lounge!'

In the back seat, Miles rolled his eyes. Journee checked the house again. The body was no longer there, it had gone. The curtains lay wide open. She was staring at nothing.

Once inside, Miles took great delight in showing off his strength by yanking the old alarm into the OFF position. He stumbled further inside. Betty froze. This time toys were splayed across the floor as if it were Christmas morning. The kitchen looked like a baby elephant had thrown a tantrum in it. There were smashed plates, broken cups, and spilt orange juice. Three pots lay on the floor.

Betty tiptoed through the kitchen and into the laundry.

'Get out of here, whoever you are!' she yelled, her voice quivering. And then she made the strangest noise, like an animal might if it was about to be attacked. 'ARGGH!' she screamed. 'Whoever you are, get out of my house! My husband is a policeman!'

The children held the back of their mother's shirt. It was wet from sweat. The front door opened. The dogs barked. Betty didn't hesitate. She snatched a broom, marched to the entrance, waited for the door to open, and thwacked the hideous, smelly criminal, who just happened to be her husband, Mr Bill Blake.

At first he didn't appear to be hurt, but almost instantly drops of blood hit the floor. Journee was mesmerised by her father's bleeding nose. She watched the blood gently trickle onto the white carpet, like raspberries on ice cream.

Betty held the broom above her head like a warrior with a spear. 'You're…early,' she said, and then realised the silly thing she'd just done. 'Sorry, I thought you were a burglar.'

'Well? I'm not!' He wiped his nose and sniffed. 'That was a…very hard hit.'

Journee tried very hard to hold in her giggle, so turned away instead.

'I said I was sorry. I was-'

'-She was scared, Dad,' said Journee.

Bill shook his head and pulled his trousers up high. He turned to his wife. 'Checked the bedrooms?' he asked. 'No sign of entry? Dogs okay?'

'Yes, no, yes.'

Bill put his hands on his hips teapot-style. 'So, if there is no obvious sign of anyone having come in, how do you explain this?' And he pointed to the mess before them.

'The house was as clean as a bean when I left this morning,' said Betty.

'Then who made the mess?' demanded Bill. 'Come on now, who was it?'

Journee's head throbbed. Her body was tense, her chest tight. 'Dad, please listen,' she said, pulling her phone from her pocket. 'I took these pictures this morning. Mum's right, the house was tidy when we left.'

Bill Blake dabbed his head gently with his fingertips. 'Well, someone around here is not telling the truth and if I find out who it is, that someone will have their phone confiscated. Do you understand?'

Miles and Journee nodded and loped to their bedroom.

Have you ever noticed the magic of music? How it can take you away from the Horrible and into the Happy? It's magic because it can make you forget those despicable things someone may have called you. Or wipe out the memory of an exploding red pen. Or a burst packet of fish food. Music is like a birthday party for your brain, especially Bob Marley played loud.

Journee wiped sticky orange juice from the kitchen floor. She tried her very best to understand how pot plants might have fallen over by themselves.

Who used the pens the day before? If someone really had broken into their home, why weren't the windows smashed? And why didn't they steal anything?

If only her father treated her as well as he treated his dogs, she could ask him about these things. But right now he was in one of his moods. Ringo and Moses lay on his lap as he picked his nose and watched the TV news.

'Burglaries! Armed robbery! And *another* missing person in Millwater?' Betty exclaimed.

'Honey, are you sure this is a safe town? We were told it was safe. And how come so many people go missing here? That's the second one this week!'

Bill picked fleas from his dogs and slurped his tea. 'It's not my fault,' he said, foraging for a lost slipper beneath the couch.

'But isn't that what your new job is, darling?

To find missing people?'

'There's other policemen in Millwater, why don't you ask them?'

As Betty stood, the doorbell rang. The man outside wore a crisp white uniform and leant on a truck with wiggly music notes and electric guitars painted on its doors.

'Mr Blake?' said the man in the uniform.

'What about it?' Bill replied.

'No need to be rude,' replied the man. 'I have your Steinway upright piano in the truck. Are you happy for my boys to bring it in? We'll need payment before we leave. It's a steal at $7,779!'

'Wrong house!' Bill bellowed. 'We've already got a piano.'

The man glanced at his clipboard. '88 Cabbage Tree Avenue?' he asked.

'Yes, but I did not order an eight-thousand-dollar piano!' said Bill.

'$7,779, sir.'

'WHO CARES if I'm twenty…twenty…' '$21 off, sir. 7,779 plus 21 equals $8000, the price you mentioned.'

Bill's nostrils flared like the doors of a tent in a storm. 'It is not my piano. I never bought one, I never ordered one,' he said. 'Now, if you don't mind I have a slipper to find!'

Bill slammed the door again and turned to find his wife smiling.

'I forgot to thank you,' she said. 'What for?' asked Bill.

'For making the bed again this morning. That's the *third* time this week.'

Bill screwed his face up and wiped sweat from his brow. 'How could I have made the bed this morning if I left the house before you?' he asked.

'Well, *someone* did,' muttered Betty, and sat down, trying to mentally retrace her steps and looking as confused as the piano-seller himself.

After dinner, Journee had the lounge all to herself. She made herself a cup of tea and was about to check her phone, but as she made her way towards the couch she heard a high-pitched squealing sound. She stopped, before following where she thought the sound was coming from. She brushed her hand across the old alarm. Journee put her ear against this rusty box on the wall. The squeals continued. Next she tried to open the alarm's door, but it didn't budge.

She tried again, this time with more force and the door finally opened.

Inside, she found what looked like some sort of nest. When she touched it, it felt like cotton wool, and was as black as night. She moved her head closer and suddenly saw something move. There were tiny white things, lots of them! Each one was no bigger than a leaf bug and they were moving. She watched in fascination as the tiny beings stood up, like miniature people! They ran about the place inside the nest. When they bumped into each other, miniscule sparks of electricity zapped and popped. Journee rubbed her eyes.

This was not possible.

She peered into the alarm cavity once more. The tiny white beings were dancing now, frolicking. She could hear squeaking sounds. She opened the door as far as it would go and peered behind the switchboard, far into the house. She was utterly fascinated. Here was a young girl so scared of spiders and cockroaches and other disgusting insects, yet when she saw these creatures she felt calm.

Suddenly, she heard a door slam. 'Fatty Vampire, you stepped on MY side of the room, I can tell because your towel's there! Keep! AWAY!' It was Miles. Journee quickly slammed the alarm door shut and walked slowly down the hallway to her room.

Hours later and Journee could barely stop thinking about what she had seen inside the alarm.

Had they been ordinary old insects it wouldn't have bothered her, or intrigued her.

But they most definitely were not insects. They were tiny *beings*.

CHAPTER 3

At breakfast, Miles almost wore himself out by trying to achieve the most realistic fart sounds possible. But Journee barely noticed, she was too transfixed by the old alarm box on the wall.

To her surprise, her day turned out to be simply wonderful, and it was all thanks to Bonnie-Kate, who had helped her during the infamous fish-food incident. Not only did Bonnie-Kate join Journee for lunch outside the school hall, she also talked about her incredibly annoying, smelly, potty-mouthed little brother. OMG, an actual friend who would listen to her own brother troubles. Journee could have hugged her!

'Do you have your own room?' Journee asked.

'Doubt it!' replied Bonnie-Kate. 'What about you?'

'Doubt it!' Journee said, laughing. 'Can I tell you something, and you promise not to laugh?'

'Of course!' Bonnie-Kate replied.

'Last night I started a list of ways to make Miles fall off the earth. Like buying a lock for my door, or making a 'BOYS NOT WELCOME' sign, or playing music he hates, really loudly. I was even going to pretend I had the flu and cough on him – on purpose!'

'Ha! Snap, I've done all of those things, literally all of them.'

'And?' 'And what?'

'Did they work?'

'Nope,' replied Bonnie-Kate, pulling a bottle out of her school bag. 'But *this* did.'

Journee glanced at the bottle. It was called 'Evening in Paris. '*Perfume*?' asked Journee.

Bonnie-Kate shrugged her shoulders and grinned. 'How badly do you want to get rid of this cretin of a brother?'

'Badly,' Journee replied.

'This stuff stinks! Spray it everywhere, every

day, every night, Miles will run a mile! And you, my friend, will get your own room.'

'Did it work for you?'

'I'm still experimenting, but it's annoying him beyond belief. Here, take a bottle.'

Journee offered her hand, before pulling it away.

'But isn't it expensive?'

'It's a gift,' replied Bonnie-Kate, grabbing Journee's hand and pulling her along the footpath.

How simply wonderful it was to find a new friend.

———

That night Journee placed the bottle in the drawer by her bedside table and fell asleep with a grin on her face. But she was woken abruptly in the early hours of the morning when rain thrashed the window above her bed. A snap of thunder followed. A door slammed.

Journee glanced at her phone. It was 1.14 a.m.

'Miles!' she whispered. 'Miles! Did you hear that?'

But nothing could have woken that boy.

Journee sat up and turned on her bedside lamp. Three small white beings stood at the foot of her bed. Each glowed white, but was also see-through, like a jellyfish.

The three white things had arms and legs, like humans, but their faces were far simpler, just two dull black eyes and a small mouth. The tallest thing was no taller than a toddler. Their bodies were slightly round in shape and each had a small wire on their head, which looked like some sort of antenna. The antenna, if that's what it was, moved from side to side and made a buzzing sound, flashing red and blue. Journee squirmed in her bed, attempting to crawl up the wall behind her.

'Miles!' She quivered and suddenly coughed as loudly and as violently as she'd ever done. Her coughing stopped. She wiped her teary eyes. The strangers were still there.

The smallest one snatched the skull-and-crossbones cap beside Journee's bed.

'Mine!' it said, quickly hiding behind the taller white things.

'What do you mean, *mine*?' she asked, too

puzzled to think. 'Who are you?'

'What's wrong with your face noise, Fuss Bucket?' asked the slightly taller white thing.

'My…my what?' Journee shrieked.

The white thing imitated Journee's cough. 'Oh…that?' Journee replied. 'I have a twisted bone in my nose. I've always had it, but the doctor told my mother it's…none of your business! WHO ARE YOU?'

The white things moved back abruptly, which gave Journee a chance to get a better look. None of the strangers wore clothes. The largest white thing wore nothing more than a watch and a gold chain. The slightly shorter one wore a scarf with roses on it and the smallest one wore the stolen cap. The cap was on backwards, like rappers often wear, a torn hole making way for the creature's antenna.

Journee was scared beyond belief, but she refused to show it. 'I *said*,' she whispered. 'Who are you and what do you want!'

The largest white thing stepped forward. 'We need help,' it said. 'Now.'

But by the time Journee swung her legs out of

bed the three things had gone.

Three hours later and Miles was fast asleep. Journee peered outside her room. Her heart raced. She wiped her sleep-dust-filled eyes. A bedroom door opened and Mr Blake stomped to the bathroom. He left the door open and whizzed for a very long time. Journee waited and waited. Finally he finished. He didn't flush. He never flushed. He didn't wash his hands either. He never washed his hands. Mr Blake groaned as he fell back into bed.

Journee crept down the hall and towards the kitchen, checking very carefully that every window was locked and every door bolted.

As she approached the kitchen, her footsteps slowed. Journee opened the fridge and grabbed a carton of milk. As she poured a glass, she heard a bump from the cupboard by the stove. She bent down and took a closer look at a rectangular shape, like the outline of a small door. She put her ear to the wall.

Another bump, followed by the sound of something beeping. Journee pulled away and stood in a hurry.

She peered down the hallway. Everyone was

fast asleep.

Her knees creaked as she bent down again and something, who knows what exactly, made her push that rectangle. When she did, it moved slightly inwards. Journee pushed it again, but it was sticky and old, just like her own bedroom door. It needed a more demanding push. This time she leant against it with all of her weight and fell sideways.

Now there was enough room to poke her head into the dark, cool space. It smelt like an old garage. She heard what sounded like footsteps running away from her.

There was a torch on the kitchen wall her father used when he sat outside with the dogs. Journee grabbed it, switched it on and squeezed through the door in her summer pyjamas.

At the top of the stairs was a tiny lamp that lead into a deep, dark abyss.

CHAPTER 4

Ever since she was a child, Journee had counted stairs. At school, in shops, and in movie theatres. The funny thing was that every house she had ever lived in had exactly thirteen. Their house in Easthollow had thirteen steps. Their house in Roseshore also had thirteen.

But these stairs were different. For some reason, these stairs never seemed to end. After number 57 Journee folded her arms to keep warm. She stopped at step number 68.

Someone was talking. More beeping. Was this a dream? Of course it was! It was the middle of the night after all, when dreams took place. This crazy dream featured a crazy child who found a hole in the kitchen wall and walked down, down, down into the earth…

Only, if this was a dream, why was Journee's left big toe throbbing? Because she stubbed it on stair number 92 and the pain that shot up her body would have woken a sleeping bear.

The voices were louder now. A yellowy glow began to light the steps below.

Pitch black turned to orangey grey. Journee no longer had to squint. Her eyes had adjusted to the deep black. There were shapes and shadows now.

More importantly, she could see where she was going. After 101 steps the staircase came to an end. The ground was flat. Ahead lay a shallow stream, filled with household rubbish. There was a frightful smell, just like Miles after he'd been in the bathroom. Journee noticed something else, too. The talking and beeping had stopped. The air was damp. Something swooped past her head. She fell to the floor and screamed.

A flying thing? This far under the earth?

Journee quickly pulled her fingers away from the filthy slush beside the stream. There was an almighty roar, which echoed around the underground like a freight train. She looked into the water and saw two bright red, menacing eyes.

Journee turned around quickly. She needed to pee. Her head pounded. Now she was scared, ridiculously so.

24, 25, 66 steps.

Even when she caught her bare leg on a sharp metal pipe she didn't stop. Those eyes: she couldn't stop thinking about those eyes.

78, 79, 80.

At the top of the stairs, she slammed the secret door and fell onto the kitchen floor.

Journee pulled the blankets up to her chin. In the morning, the first thing she noticed when she rolled out of bed were her legs. One ached badly, the other sported a scratch covered in dried blood. It had really happened, she thought to herself.

Last night really happened.

As she hobbled to the kitchen she studied the rectangular shape by the bench. It was still slightly open. Betty served up leftover pancakes and cream, which seemed a little too runny.

'Good morning, gorgeous!' said Betty, kissing

Journee's forehead.

Miles chose his own culinary masterpiece over pancakes, opting for three different cereals in one bowl before adding chocolate milk, peanut butter and raspberry jam.

'Going to Hugo's today.' He grinned at Journee. 'Gonna drink beer.'

'That's nice,' replied Journee, rubbing her lower leg.

'Hey, got a joke,' he said, and pushed his bowl away. 'There's this teacher and she says to the class, 'What does a shoe shop give you?'

'Shoes,' Journee replied.

'Correct! And what does a hen give you?'

'Eggs.'

'Correct! And what does a big fat cow give you?'

Journee waited for the answer.

'Homework! Cos it's the teacher, she's the big fat cow and she gave homew-'

'I get it, Miles!' snapped Journee. 'Do you know how a joke works? Do you? *You* say the punch line and the person, in this case, *me*, works it out. If it's funny, I laugh. Get it?'

Miles continued to talk, Journee knew so because her ears were infected with non-stop blubbery nonsense, but right now something far more important had piqued her interest. She could not stop staring at the secret door beside the kitchen cupboard.

That night Journee lay wide awake thinking about strange, naked white blobs. Who were they? Where did they come from? Would they ever come back? And why didn't they wear pants?

Speaking of which, she needed to pee. On went her comfy woollen slippers and she crept to the bathroom. She even took her phone, which she knew was a risk because she'd been told a hundred times that she was only allowed to own one if she promised to turn it off one hour before bedtime. But it was late, and no one was up. Who would ever know?

Just as Journee was about to sit on the toilet…
'You betrayed us, Fuss Bucket.'

Wham! Journee stood so abruptly she tripped on her pyjama pants and landed face first on the floor. She saw the white thing in the mirror. It was the smallest one with the baseball cap.

'Really?' Journee shrieked. 'I'm in the bathroom! How long have you been there?'

'Fuss Buckets are liars,' said the white thing. 'We even left the door open so you knew where to go. Do you know how hard it was to come up here in the middle of the night and ask for help?'

'I tried. Look!' Journee replied, pointing to the scratch on her leg.

'You betrayed us, Fuss Bucket!'

'Stop calling me that. My name is Journee.

Journee Blake. And I never said I would help you. I tried, honestly, but I ran straight home when I saw these two giant red eyes-'

'-Eye-Shiner!' said the small white thing.

Journee flushed the toilet, but only so her parents wouldn't hear anybody speaking. She moved closer to the white thing's dull black eyes. '*Eye-Shiner?*' she asked.

'What you saw was an Eye-Shiner,' said the small white thing. 'Flat snout, long tail, scales.'

'A…*crocodile?*' Journee asked.

'I think that's what Fuss Buckets call them.'

'Wait,' Journee continued. 'You're saying

there's a crocodile beneath our house?'

The white thing nodded. Journee shook her head and laughed. The white thing stepped forward, the lights on its head glowing like a Christmas tree.

'It is the most dangerous Eye-Shiner in under the world. Now stop wasting time. Follow me.'

Bang, bang, bang came the knock on the bathroom door.

'Journee, is that you?' It was the unmistakable voice of her dad. 'You'd better not be on that phone.' The door suddenly flew open and Journee was standing just inches from her father.

'Dad, it's nothing,' she said, terribly worried she no longer had a secret. 'I was just talking to…' But as she turned around, there was nothing there. 'Um…'

Mr Blake spied the phone on the floor.

'You're on your *phone*?' he enquired. 'At *this* time? In *here*?' He raised an eyebrow. He picked up the phone and waved it about in the air. 'One week.'

'Huh?' Journee replied, her mind in a muddle, mostly concerned about the disappearance of the little white blob.

'Confiscated for one week,' continued Bill

Blake. 'I've told you a thousand times not to take your phone into the bathroom. It's called *hygiene.* Do you know that when I was in the army we had to wash-'

'-Okay, sure, Dad,' Journee said, peering around the bathroom feverishly. 'Sorry. Sorry, Dad.'

But he had already left.

With her door slightly ajar, Journee could hear her father groan and fall into bed. Apart from the snoring, the only noise was the low hum of the fridge.

She collected the torch off the wall, then snatched some scissors. She replaced the scissors with a knife, which was far too big and far too sharp for any child to use.

What was she doing? Was she *mad?* Who on earth would follow an unknown white being underground? Yet something made Journee Blake push the secret door once more.

On the other side the small white thing stood to attention, like a small white soldier.

'About time!' it said. 'Let's proceed.'

'Wait,' said Journee. 'I don't even know your name.'

'Chime,' said the small white thing, and ate

what looked like a dead fly.

'Chime? Oh, okay, well, hi, Chime,' said Journee. 'Now listen, I'm supposed to be asleep. Tell me where we're going exactly and what time we'll be back. Do we need food? Shouldn't I be wearing socks and shoes? And what if we get lost? Will we get into trouble if anyone-'

'-Less talk, more walk, Fuss Bucket,' it said. 'But I don't even know why I'm helping you!' Journee replied.

Chime bounded down the slippery steps, four at a time. 'Because you like mud tea!' said the small white thing. 'And Memory makes the best mud tea under the world.'

Chime took Journee's hand and bounced towards a filthy brown stream filled with household rubbish. She stopped at the water's edge and kicked a soggy cereal packet.

'The Loopoopaloopoo,' said Chime, peering over Journee's shoulder.

'It smells like Miles,' said Journey.

'Yes, it's a sewer,' Chime replied. 'You do know what a sewer is?'

Journee thought very carefully before answering,

'Isn't it where all the-'

'Foo-foo ends up!' Chime replied. 'Foo-foo?'

'When Fuss Buckets sit on the squeeze seat in your bathroom and flush this is where all the foo-foo-'

'I got it,' said Journee, holding her nose and squinting. 'It…stinks.'

'Underers can't smell the smell!' 'Underers?'

'Yes, us! Underers can't smell any smell. It's one of our many powers, along with binocular vision and photographic memory. We also speak 9,146 languages.'

'Oh,' said Journee, and wondered if her new accomplice might also help with homework.

101 steps later the land was flat. Journee hesitated as she leant over a slow-moving stream. The red eyes weren't here tonight. Chime stomped through household rubbish and Journee followed, her woolly slippers getting soggier by the second.

Through cramped tunnels they went, where stalactites hung from the ceiling like giant fingers.

Water dripped from the ceiling and the atmosphere, so stale, so dank, felt as if the air was thousands of years old.

There was a high-pitched squeal above. Journee froze, before directing the glow of the torch to the cave's roof. Hundreds of bats peered down at her, their wings wrapped around their bodies like shiny cloaks. The big, black beasts took off as quick as insects, swooping and swerving through the tight, twisted alleyways of the underground.

Journee felt a splotch land on her shoulder, and then another. She got an almighty shock to find Chime standing behind her, pointing to the fresh splotches.

'Guano,' said the small white thing. 'Guano?' Journee replied.

Chime pointed to the bats above. 'From them.'

It's a funny thing how the thought of more bat poo landing on your shoulder can make you run twice as fast as usual. Journee saw Chime up ahead, but why on earth was she following her?

Where was she going? Who *were* these things?

And what if something terrible happened?

Who would even find them down here?

Suddenly she felt her arm being tugged by something. It was Chime, who pointed to a dimly-lit cave ahead. Two white glowing heads with black beady eyes stared back at them.

But instead of being terrified, Journee breathed a sigh of relief. She'd already met these white things. One wore the pretty scarf, and the other the sparkly gold chain.

'Hi…again.' She waved meekly.

Suddenly the white thing with the gold chain burst through the cave's door. 'Beep off, Jughead!' it said. 'You have no permission to enter a fully programmable zone.' A rainbow laser beam shot out from its belly and coated Journee in a spray of colour.

'No!' said Chime. 'This is the trusted Fuss Bucket, remember!'

The white thing with the gold chain was now just millimetres from Journee's face. 'Your status,' he said. 'What is it?'

'My *status*?' Journee asked, suddenly covered in multi-coloured fluorescent dust. She turned to Chime for guidance.

'What do Fuss Buckets call you?' it demanded.

'*Fuss Buckets?*' Journee asked.

'Fuss Buckets. You lot! Two-legged beings who rush about and fuss. What is your status?'

'Oh, my *name?*' Journee said. 'Journee Blake.'

The thing began to laugh and couldn't stop. It snorted and guffawed and shook. Then it became very serious indeed. 'Tell any other Fuss Bucket you saw us and I will personally tie you up in Burglar's Alley.'

'Burglar's what?' Journee asked, and noticed she was beginning to itch all over.

In a rush she felt very oozy, as if she was having trouble waking from a very long sleep. Ten seconds later weariness overtook her. She lay down on a nearby rock. How comfortable this rock was, like a pillow. She fell into a deep, pleasant slumber.

The cave was no bigger than Journee's bedroom at home. There was a large rock that doubled as a table, and three other irregular-sized boulders for seats. This is exactly the spot where she woke to find the three white things beeping at each other.

Beep, beep, beep went the white things, over and over.

'Ahem,' said Journee, letting everyone know she was awake.

Suddenly the two larger white things scuttled away to the other side of the cave. They held each other tight, as if Journee was a frightful monster, or a gigantic tidal wave.

'Mum, it's fine, she's not going to hurt anyone,' said Chime, and took Journee by the hand and walked her towards the others. 'Let me introduce you.' She patted the friendly-looking one with the scarf and said, 'This is my mum, Memory.' Chime moved towards the other white thing. 'And this is my dad, Panic.'

'Panic?' Journee asked.

'Yes, *Panic*, you got a Fuss Bucket problem with that?'

'Dad, politeness, remember?' said Chime. 'You already know Journee Blake, the Fuss Bucket from upstairs. And she's not fond of bat excrement.'

'Excrement?' Journee replied. 'Poo!' said Chime.

'Oh, that? No, I'm most certainly not!' said Journee.

Yet no one in the cave seemed to laugh, or

even say anymore after Journee's reply. The only sound was the drip, drip, drip of brown water from the cave's rocky ceiling.

No one moved, apart from the white thing with the scarf who shuffled ever so slowly towards her. It was as if she were a dog that might bite at any second.

Soon the white thing was within arm's reach of Journee. The girl studied its tiny black eyes and glowing, yet almost see-through body.

Now the white thing's nose was almost touching Journee's! The poor girl froze. What was she to do? There was nowhere to run. Was this thing going to hurt her? Did it have secret powers?

'Your head is sore,' said the white thing with the scarf.

Yes, it did have secret powers because Journee's head ached and throbbed. Suddenly she felt very calm. 'How…how did you know?'

'Panic should never have fired the rainbow laser beam. Sometimes he forgets who he's met and who he hasn't. It's not his fault. He was programmed badly.'

'A…rainbow laser beam?' Journee asked.

At the very mention of the word, Panic fired another one, only this time the multi-coloured stream of smoke flew directly through the cave's window.

'Enough!' said Memory, who placed her hand on Journee's, which was very much like a warm laptop. 'I'm so sorry about that, dear. Please join us for mud tea.'

'Affirmative!' yelled Chime.

The cave was even colder now and insects crawled up the walls. There was a whiff of wet clay and everywhere you walked there was a squelchy sound beneath your foot. Memory handed Journee a very familiar-looking *Simpsons* coffee mug. Inside was a dirt-brown, gluggy mixture with twigs, stones and a big, fat live worm.

'Mud tea!' said Chime, who slurped hers as if it were chocolate milk with marshmallows.

Journee smiled through gritted teeth, as any polite guest would. Then she told a big fat lie. 'I'll try it when it cools down a bit,' she said, accidentally knocking the mug over on purpose.

Only then did Journee realise how noisy her

own world was. In her world above ground dogs barked and buses honked. But down here there was nothing.

Which you'd think might be lovely and calm, but to Journee the silence was frightening.

Chime placed an old cushion next to Journee, but she was too polite to say it was like sitting on an enormous wet sponge. She took another look around the cave and wondered how any person, or Fuss Bucket, or white blob could live here.

In the corner of the cave Panic laid a dirt old blanket on a jagged rock. A cereal box stuffed with rubbish was placed on top. The two older Underers were laughing.

'Why are they laughing?' asked Journee. 'Your clothes,' Chime replied.

'What about my clothes?' 'You're wearing them!'

Memory dusted the rock and cuddled beside Chime. Journee studied the older Underer's perfectly smooth white face, which had the appearance of an animated balloon. How bizarre, yet wonderful to meet someone so strange, so unreal.

Memory opened a page of the book and smiled at Journee. 'You may be a little too old for this story,' she said. 'But it helps Chime get to sleep. Maybe you'll like it too. I hope so.'

Journee crept forward and studied the book's front cover. That book did not belong to the Underers, it belonged to her. It was *Charlotte's Web*, and she knew it was her copy because the pig on the front cover had a moustache and silly hat drawn on it, which Miles did one night when he was angry at Journee for using his *Power Rangers* towel.

As the candlelight flickered, Journee watched Memory's peaceful face as she read *Charlotte's Web*, her speech like a song. She thought how beautifully serene it was down here. No annoying brothers. No yelling father. No attention-seeking dogs.

Soon the chapter came to an end. At that very second, Journee discovered it was five o'clock in the morning.

'I've got to go!' she said, scuttling towards the 101 steps. Before she took off completely she looked back at the cave. 'That *Simpsons* mug?' said Journee. 'That's from our kitchen, isn't it?'

The Underers nodded, appearing a little embarrassed.

'Do you guys know anything about the mess in our house?' Journee asked. 'You know, the one I've been getting the blame for?'

The Underers nodded.

'What exactly do you know about my family?' Journee asked.

Memory licked her lips and mud tea dripped down her snow-white chest. 'You have a piano and two dogs, and your dad is a policeman,' she said. 'But not a very good one.'

The three white things giggled as Journee left. She did too.

CHAPTER 5

The next morning when the Blake family left for school and work the Underers settled into 88 Cabbage Tree Avenue. It was their favourite time of day, when they had a Fuss Bucket's house all to themselves.

Memory was busy gliding about the house as if she were dancing on a Broadway stage. Panic set about making every bed in the house. He had always been the tidiest Underer, unlike Chime who seemed to create havoc and mess wherever she went. Her new favourite trick was to change the language settings on the TV from English to Chinese with the aerial on her head.

Once the beds were made, Panic sat below the alarm sensor in the lounge, making sure it stayed flashing red at all times.

Suddenly he spotted a black cat outside the kitchen window. He effortlessly sprung onto the bench. 'Sneakabout, it's a Sneakabout!' he yelled. 'Everyone out!'

The cat glanced up at the strange see-through creature, which was flicking its tail in the air playfully.

'Panic, he can't come in, remember?' said Memory. 'There is no Sneakabout door.'

'But if he does? If he did!' Panic said. 'He can't,' Memory replied.

'But if he does the wee-woo-wee-woo will go off and we-'

'-I know what will happen,' said Memory. 'But he can't get in. And if the Sneakabout can't get in we are safe to enjoy these.'

And Memory passed Panic a plate of fresh chocolate brownies. Panic munched the brownies as quickly as possible. Then he turned his attention to the dogs outside the back door.

Memory said, 'And they can't come in either, remember?'

'But if they did!' Panic replied. 'The wee-woo-wee-woo would go off-'

'-Ringo and Moses don't have a key, dear,' said Memory. 'And anyway dogs can't unlock doors with their paws.'

'HA!' said Panic. 'A joke, a play on words, a rib-tickler. I enjoyed it. It was funny.' He then shot an insect on the kitchen floor into a hundred pieces with his giant rainbow laser beam.

'Dad, don't waste all your shots,' said Chime. 'We might need them.'

At exactly 3.12 p.m. Journee squeezed past wet, overgrown weeds on the path alongside the house.

She unstuck the sticky old gate, and grabbed the door key from under the mat.

This was no dream. Her mind had not been playing tricks on her.

Through the window in the back door she saw them. The white blobs. In her house! But instead of going inside, she decided to watch them in secret.

It was Memory she saw first, seated at the piano. Because of her short stature, the Underer needed two cushions to reach the keys, which did not stop her playing the most beautiful tunes. Chime was nearby, shovelling freshly baked brownies into her mouth.

Twelve at a time! Incredible! It was almost superhuman. Did she tidy up? Of course she didn't.

Hundreds of crumbs and leftover biscuits littered the kitchen floor.

And books, too. Panic was reading those, pulling one after the other down from the shelves in the lounge. He flicked through each for a few seconds, or less, before putting it down, picking up another and doing the same. Surely he wasn't reading like that?

Did he tidy up? Hm, well you know the answer to that.

Journee continued to watch from her secret spying position. She felt so wonderfully proud to have discovered such a secret, the sort of secret every child at school would love to know.

But they couldn't have it. It was all hers. And she wasn't going to tell a soul.

Fifteen minutes later, Journee couldn't wait any longer. She quickly unlocked the back door and approached the alarm pad. She heard a *pip-pip* noise, like the sound of a microwave beeping when your meal is ready. Of course, Journee thought to herself. This was when she was supposed to remember to switch the arm of the alarm from ON to OFF.

The *pip-pip* noise kept going. And now…

WEE-WOO-WEE-WOO!

WEE-WOO-WEE- WOO!

The alarm was spewing out the most distressing screech, like a police siren having an argument with an ambulance. Or ten thousand children stubbing their toe at once. Journee's ears pounded and throbbed, but the white blobs themselves were in far worse shape.

As the alarm shrieked, all three of them changed colour almost instantly, from snow white, to sickly yellow, to deathly grey. She watched as Panic threw Chime on his shoulder and struggled towards the secret door. Next he helped Memory, who had fallen from the piano stool and lay weak on the lounge floor.

The father white blob, who just minutes before had had the energy of a sprightly teenager, was now bent over and as exhausted as a one-hundred-year-old man. With one last heave, Panic dragged Memory and Chime through the secret door.

Journee was panicking now. *The alarm! Switch it off!* The poor girl dropped to her knees. When she pulled herself up she sped across to the screeching alarm and tried to yank the arm to the OFF position, but it became jammed and too tight to move. Journee threw her body force behind it and with all her might heaved the arm anti-clockwise.

She felt a click.

WEE-Woo-wee-wo… Silence.

She scrambled to her feet. Just as she was about to follow the Underers, someone unlocked the front door. It was her mum.

'Oh, darling, another mess,' she said. 'Come on, let's clean this up before your father gets home.'

Journee drew in a deep breath, wiping the sweat from her brow. 'Okay, mum,' she replied. 'Thank you.'

CHAPTER 6

Journee sat on her bed, her ears still ringing. She was confused. What had she done wrong? What made the Underers react like they did? How could they have been so happy one second, and collapsing the next. Why did they turn *yellow?*

She thought back to when the alarm was at its noisiest, when the white blobs could barely walk. If Panic hadn't been there, what would have happened to Memory and Chime?

Perhaps it was something she said? Maybe she wasn't supposed to surprise them? So the next day she snuck home even earlier and knocked on the back door loudly.

'Hi!' she said. 'It's me, the, what do you call it,

Fuss Bucket?'

But the exact same thing happened. The Underers took one look at her and escaped to the secret door. They each acted as if they had seen something so frightening, so horrific, that their only hope was to run for their lives.

It happened three days in a row.

Journee knew exactly what was happening. Her world was crumbling again. She cursed herself for being so stupid. How *stupid* to think these things, these white blobs, were any different to anyone else she had ever met. It was just like school all over again.

The next morning Journee felt glum. She wouldn't have been surprised if no one spoke to her at school, so was understandably over the moon when Bonnie-Kate sidled up beside her and offered her half a cream donut.

'Well?' Bonnie-Kate asked, devouring her half.

'Well what?' Journee replied.

'You haven't said anything about your brainless brother, so I can only assume my plan worked. He's moved rooms? No, even better, he's moved *houses?*' 'Um…it's just a bit complicated,

Bonnie-Kate,'

Journee replied.

'Duh! I know! Brothers *are*.'

Journee smiled and looked into Bonnie-Kate's eyes, they were blue and sparkly and bursting with life. Could she be trusted? What an awful thought. But *could* she? Would Journee achieve anything by talking about what was really happening in her house?

'You haven't even *tried* the perfume, have you? Be honest.'

Journee shook her head. She was dying to tell her friend her secret, and the truth very nearly spilt out, but the bell rang.

Bonnie-Kate sprung up and threw her donut wrapper into the bin. 'Promise me you'll do it tonight! Tell me tomorrow what happened. Promise?'

Journee nodded and began walking in the opposite direction. 'Thank you for the donut.' 'No probs! See ya!' replied Bonnie-Kate, bouncing towards her classroom.

Journee arrived home and stood at the door. She took a deep breath. Once inside, she heard the warning pips of the alarm and yanked the machine's arm into the OFF position.

Miles arrived home next and interrupted Journee as she was getting dressed in their room. 'EW, YUCK!' he screamed. 'Do that somewhere else!'

'GO AWAY!' Journee replied, and slammed the door.

Later that night when Miles was fast asleep Journee opened her top drawer. The 'Evening in Paris' perfume was gone. He would pay for this in the morning, she decided.

Soon, Journee fell into a deep slumber and woke to find a small glowing light at the end of her bed.

She rubbed her eyes and sat up quickly. It was Chime, who stood there with her arms folded, looking very cross indeed.

'Do we *smell*?' asked Chime. 'That's it, isn't it? We *smell*.'

'Huh?' whispered Journee.

'You don't visit us anymore!' said Chime. 'You think we smell.'

'Well, where you *live* smells, but you don't smell too bad, I suppose.'

'Good, because I thought we were supposed to be friends.'

'I've wanted to see you all week!' said Journee. 'I even came home early.'

'Exactly the problem,' Chime replied. 'What is?'

'Coming home early without telling us.'

Chime moved in closer, so close that Journee could feel her sweet breath. 'You must warn us if you're going to come into the house when the wee-woo-wee-woo is set.'

'The what?'

'The wee-woo-wee-woo.'

'What's a wee-woo-wee-woo?' Journee asked.

'The wee-woo-wee-woo!'

'*What's* a wee-woo-wee-woo?'

'An alarm, I think is what Fuss Buckets call it.'

'So why do I need to warn you if I come home early?'

'In case you can't turn it off, like the day the wee-woo-wee-woo went off. If the wee-woo-wee-woo ever goes off when we are inside your house, like it did when you were there, it might be curtains for us. We would get very sick, very quick. We might even be zooped completely.'

'You'd…*die?*'

The small Underer nodded. 'Yes, but don't be such a morbid Fuss Bucket. Get dressed, Memory's made fresh mud tea.'

Down the slippery steps to the misty underground went Journee and Chime, which was exactly the moment raisins starting falling from above. Raisins! From the sky!

Only, when Journee looked closer, she discovered they weren't raisins at all. Raisins did not dissolve when you brushed them off your shoulder. Journee smelt her hand and shuddered.

More guano.

She wiped her hands on her jeans in disgust and turned quickly to climb the stairs back to the kitchen. But soon the mist cleared and Journee found herself somewhere very familiar.

It was Chime's home.

Within seconds Panic was inches from her face.

He paused for an uncomfortably long time.

'Beep off, Jughead!' he said. 'You have no permission to enter a fully programma-'

'Not again, Dad?' replied Chime. 'It's Journee, the trusted Fuss Bucket.'

Panic walked to the corner of the cave, mumbling to himself. And there he picked up a bottle that Journee recognised. Was that her 'Evening in Paris?' She watched as he began spraying perfume all over himself.

'Hey!' said Journee. 'That's my-' '-Borrowing it!' said Panic.

Journee frowned. 'But…how did you know where… Oh, it really *does* stink!'

'Thank you,' replied Panic, hands on hips like a supermodel.

'It's not a compliment.'

'It's not a *what?*' Panic replied, spraying his whole body with the stuff.

'It doesn't matter,' Journee replied, and felt an arm on her shoulder. It was Memory, but unlike Chime, her face was deadly serious, like a headmaster about to hand out a severe punishment. 'You don't need to say anything, Mum,' said Chime. 'I already told her.'

'Told me what?' Journee asked.

'About the wee-woo-wee-woo?' Chime whispered.

'Oh, *that?*' Journee replied. 'I'm *so* sorry. It's just, I couldn't remember the code and-'

'-It's a little confusing, I understand,' said Memory, her voice calm and friendly. 'But next time, you must tell us if you come home early. Our family is born of the Underer 600 alarm, you might have seen it, by your front and back door. This alarm must be activated for us to be in your house. If it rings, like the day you came home and forgot the code, it will be very sad times for us.'

'We get sick, Sick Face!' said Panic. We die, Die Face!'

'Dad, please, 'said Chime. 'I already told her.' 'I'm so sorry,' Journee said. 'I…I just panicked… All I saw was you trying to get out.'

Memory placed her hand on Journee's. It was dry, like the body of a snake. 'Life is not easy for Underers, dear,' she said. 'There are countless dangers above and below ground that can end it for all of us.'

'Like it did for Flash,' said Chime.

'Yes, Chime, as it did for poor wee Flash.'
'Flash?' Journee asked.

Panic poured himself more mud tea and slurped it quickly. Some of it spilt onto his clear white body, which seemed to neither hurt nor faze him.

'Another time,' said Memory, as if trying to think of something else very quickly. 'But let's not be sad! Popper pie, anyone?'

'Poppers', Journee soon learnt, were what Fuss Buckets knew as rats. And Underers had a very good reason for hating them. There were stories of Poppers actually popping Underers as they slept. Imagine that! One minute you're dreaming about mud tea and the next some nasty buck-toothed critter has popped you like a giant pimple.

'I catch 'em and cook 'em!' Panic said, meat dripping from the pastry of his pie.

Memory scooped more pie onto another plate Journee recognised from her own kitchen.

'Every Popper in a pie is one that can't pop us!' she said.

Journee watched from the laundry doorway as

Miles played with his pet tarantula. It really was a disgusting creature, a scary, hairy beast which thankfully never left its cage.

'I know you're there,' said Miles. 'I can hear you breathing.'

'Very funny,' Journee replied.

'Come in and say hello to my little buddy.'
'Never,' said Journee, folding her arms tightly, trying her very best not to think about the night Miles played a very dirty trick on her. She'd just finished reading a chapter of *Charlotte's Web* and pulled the fresh sheets up to her chin. As she closed her eyes she felt something tickle her toes. At first she laughed. What was it, she wondered. Suddenly the thing crept up her leg. She yanked back the covers and watched in horror as the tarantula scuttled up her body, like a lizard across hot sand. The spider clung to her and wouldn't let go. Its needle-like fangs dug into her skin. She had to use her bare hands to pick it off.

Then the bloodthirsty vampire clung to her arm and wouldn't let go! Betty must have heard the piercing screams because she ran into the bedroom with a glass of water and threw it over the spider, which fell to the ground and landed on its back.

Miles lay on the floor laughing. That night Journee didn't sleep, not for a minute.

Now as she looked at her brother, an incredible feeling of power came over her. Spiders were nothing compared to what she had discovered. Her brother thought he was so clever with that pathetic thing trapped in a glass cage. But she had found something no one else had ever seen. She grinned and Miles couldn't help but notice.

'What do you want anyway?' he asked.

'Oh, you know,' Journee replied. 'Just waiting for a friend.'

He stopped what he was doing. '*Friend?*' 'Yes, friend.'

'*You?*'

'Yes, me.'

'Is she stupid? Or dumb? Which one?' 'Ha, ha,' she replied and perked up like a

meerkat when she heard the doorbell ring. She ran towards it, but slowed down so as not to appear too keen.

Bonnie-Kate stood on the doorstep with her

ukulele. 'Hi,' she said, and walked right in.

What followed was what any child goes through when a new friend walks into their house. Is my house tidy enough, or big enough? What if my friend gets bored? Or judges me?

What if Mum and Dad *embarrass* me?

Journee needn't have worried. Her mum was in her room working on her new business. Sadly, Waterproof karaoke had been gazumped by an idea she called Night Builders. Betty Blake was going to employ builders to work only at night, when people were asleep! That way, she said, they could work twenty-four hours a day and complete a house in half the time! Mr Blake said that the reason builders *didn't* build at night was because of the noise, which was the exact moment Betty told everyone about her other new invention: silent hammers! As usual, Journee wished her mum good luck.

Betty got to work while Miles played video games in his bedroom, which meant the girls had the whole place to themselves. Journee found her safe place, the kitchen.' Let's make brownies,' she said, pulling ingredients from the cupboard. 'I make the best ones. Trust me, you won't be able to stop at just one.'

'I'll be the judge of that!' replied Bonnie-Kate. 'Anyway, I can't bake!'

'And I can't play a musical instrument,' said Journee.

'Well,' said Bonnie-Kate, finding a seat at the breakfast bar. 'Why don't I serenade you while you make brownies? You like Bob Marley, right?'

'Love Bob Marley!'

But as Journee began making her world-famous brownies, something worried her. What if Bonnie- Kate asked about the strange noises behind the cupboard? Was *this* the right time to say something?

Thankfully, Bonnie-Kate was so easy to talk to, and so funny. The girls chatted about anything and everything. What an afternoon, what a success! Soon, the brownies in the oven filled the house with a delicious aroma. There would even be leftovers.

And Journee knew exactly who they were for.

The next afternoon Journee ran home from school as fast as her legs would carry her. After a really horrible day, she was crying so much she could barely see where she was going. Once she reached the front doorstep she dropped her school bag and squeezed down the side of the house. Just like last time, she unstuck the sticky old gate and knocked four times on her bedroom window.

'Miss Awesome!' said Chime, dancing across from the other side of the room.

Journee wiped her eyes and looked longingly at her new friend. 'Miss *Awesome*?' she asked.

'My new name for you,' said Chime. 'Because you're awesome! We saw the note at the top of the stairs and went to where you said the brownies were hidden. OMG! Those brownies.'

'I'm glad you liked them.'

'Therefore, you're now Miss Awesome.'

'I'll be sure to make them again,' she said, and felt the warmth of doing something for someone else.

Journee studied Chime's perfectly smooth white face, which had the appearance of an animated balloon.

'You know you can't come in?' said Chime. 'Because of the wee-woo-wee-woo,' said Journee, and for the first time noticed beautiful music coming from down the hallway.

'How did Memory learn to play so well?' Journee asked.

'YouTube!' said Chime. 'Underers have photographic memories.'

Seconds later the music stopped and Memory stood behind Chime at the window.

'Hello, dear,' she said. 'What a ray of sunshine you are. How was your day?'

'Honestly?' Journee asked.

'Of course, honestly.' Memory smiled.

'My day was horrible,' said Journee. 'First of all my school bag didn't close properly and everything fell onto the floor. Pens and paper and books and lip gloss and hair ties and tissues.'

'But that's not the worst bit. Our classroom gets really stuffy because none of the windows open properly. I took my sweater off, but when I pulled it over my head everyone cracked up laughing. I looked at the ground and saw why. Somehow Miles' *Power Rangers underpants* had got stuck to the inside of my sweater, probably because they were in the dryer together, and the underpants fell onto the floor. Onto my *feet.*'

'Oh dear,' said Memory.

'It gets worse,' Journee continued. 'Then Seb Grommit snatched the underpants and waved them in the air like a cowboy with a lasso. He yelled, 'We got ourselves a superhero! She wears her undies on the outside!'

'Life is easier when you don't wear clothes,' said Chime.

'The underpants *stuck* to the ceiling fan,' Journee said. 'They spun round and round and everyone laughed. Then Miss Carboni must have suddenly remembered she was an adult and told everyone to sit down, and that's when Seb Grommit found the switch for the ceiling fan.'

'No!' said Memory.

'Yes!' said Journee. 'He switched the fan onto the fastest setting and the underpants went round even faster. Miss Carboni just sat there! The underpants shot like a bullet across the room and landed on the tallest window, the one no one can reach, not even with a ladder. They're still stuck there, even now, everyone in Room 5 can see my brother's *Power Rangers* underpants. I asked Miss Carboni if I was allowed to go to sick bay and I ran all the way home.'

'It sounds like our friend here needs some cheering up,' said Memory.

'Can I show her our prisoners?' Chime asked. 'Please! Please! Please!'

'Okay, then, just this once,' said Memory.

And just like that, Journee was dragged along the muddy paths beneath her own home, through tight alleyways and dark holes, all the while trying her best to stay close to her guide.

'Where are we going?' Journee asked, pretending not to be frightened.

'Less talk, more walk!' came Chime's reply. 'Keep your eyes open and don't stand in foo-foo.'

'Foo-foo?' Journee said. 'Chime? Tell me we're not actually running *through* foo-foo?' 'Aren't Fuss Buckets dis-gusting?' Chime replied. 'This is where all of *your* foo-foo ends up, from the squeeze seat in your bathroom!' 'Yes, well, how do *you* go to the toilet?'

With that Chime spewed out a big blob of multi- coloured goo. 'One hole in, one hole out!' she replied. 'And it's always rainbow.'

'What's always rainbow?' asked Journee. 'Whatever comes out!'

'I think I'm going to be sick,' said Journee. 'You asked, Miss Awesome!'

Just ahead, there was the sound of yelling and screaming.

'Don't worry,' said Chime, looking deeply into Journee's eyes. 'They're chained up.'

Journee crept slightly backwards. '*What* are chained up?' she asked.

She felt her hand being tugged. Around the next bend the yelling got louder. Journee could see them now. Four tattooed individuals wearing leather jackets stood chained together along the walls of the underground.

'LOOKIE HERE!' said the first burglar. 'GHOST GIRL AND A LITTLE FAT TROLL!'

'Talk like that and you'll never be free,' Chime replied.

Another burglar spat on the ground and shook mud and sweat from his long hair.

'AS IF THAT WILL EVA HAPPEN! YOU'SE WHITE BLOBS ARE M-MEANIES!'

Chime placed her hands on her hips. 'Maybe you shouldn't have stolen things from innocent people in the first place.'

'WHO'S THAT NEW PORK CHOP WIT YA? SHE'S NO WHITE BLOB!'

Chime gently pushed Journee towards the burglars. They smelt awful.

'I'm…Journee, she offered. 'Journee Blake.'

'PORK CHOP, GET US OUTTA HERE. PLEAAAASE! I'LL STEAL ANYTHING YOU WANT! MAYBE A CAR OR A PUPPY. OR CIGARETTES?

'I don't smoke,' said Journee. 'And I definitely don't steal.'

'WOOLLY WOOFTA!' replied the burglar. 'HOPE YOU FALL DOWN A DRAINPIPE AND GET EATEN BY A GAZILLION RATS!'

Journee felt herself being steered away by Chime, past one dirty face to the next.

'These are not very nice people,' said Journee. 'Well, they *are* burglars,' said Chime.

'But aren't you scared? What if they escape? Imagine what they would do to you. And isn't it a bit mean keeping them tied up like this?'

'Come,' said Chime, pulling Journee back to where they came from. 'Show you a trick.'

Seeing the two return created much excitement with the burglars, who thought they were going to be released. But Chime had other plans.

'Watch this.' She winked at Journee.

She leant in towards the largest, smelliest burglar, her face inches from a nose which resembled a parrot's beak. The burglar attempted to head-butt the Underer, but the chains were too strong and he was forced against the rock wall. Journee watched as Chime undid those chains, so his hands were free but his legs were not. The burglar now stood free.

'Are you crazy?!' Journee screamed.

'You've got a big bogey up your nose,' Chime said to the burglar. 'It's the size of a CABBAGE!'

The burglar wasted no time in utilising his good fortune. He punched Chime as hard as he could. But instead of hurting her, his fist bounced back, making the noise of a cartoon pogo stick.

Ba-boing! Ba-boing!

Chime smiled at Journee. 'Handy, huh?'

Beep! Beep! The alarm came from Journee's watch, which she always set ten minutes before school day ended. Which meant it was 2.50 p.m.

Which also meant – five minutes to get home.

Journee saw them, those red eyes in the water again. Red, glowing, terrifying eyes. Only this time the animal lifted its head above the water, showing off dozens of sharp teeth. It slowly lowered its gigantic head and began to swim away. The only parts of its body above the surface now were its snout, eyes and tail, the tip of which looked like tiny peaks of a mountain.

CHAPTER 7

Journee knelt on the other side of the kitchen cupboard, her ear against the secret door. She yanked it open and fell backwards when it finally became unstuck.

Phew, the kitchen was empty.

Journee wiped dirt from her hands and crept slowly to her bedroom. Her mum walked towards her with a basket full of clean laundry. 'Ah, there you are, darling!' said Betty. 'Where have you been? I was worried.'

Journee felt a finger prod her in the back. It was Miles.

'I tried to find you after school!' he said. 'I could have been kidnapped by aliens and tortured and thrown down a black hole and died. Then how would you have felt?'

'*Aliens?*' Journee asked.

Betty placed the washing basket at her feet.

'Where *are* my bras? There's not a single bra in here!' She looked up at Journee. 'Where were you, honey?'

'I…walked home,' said Journee. 'A different way.'

'Through a giant cobweb by the looks of it,' Betty giggled.

'Huh?' Journee asked.

'You're covered in spider webs,' said Betty. 'Looks like you've spent the day underground. Go and shower.'

'Ha! Shame!' Miles said 'You've got bird turd on your shoulder!'

Journee glanced at the guano. 'So I have,' she said, and skipped towards her bedroom like a lamb on a bouncy castle.

The next day the *Power Rangers* underpants were still there, and Seb Grommit sure let the class know all about it. But at least this time when she arrived home Journee knew exactly what to do. She knocked on the window and watched the Underers leave through the secret door behind the kitchen cupboard. Once the last one was safely through, she rammed the alarm's arm to OFF.

Phew.

Through the other side she found Memory standing at the top of the steps. Chime was wearing a very familiar-looking bright red bra, but she was so small that it drooped downwards, hanging loosely.

She pushed her chest out and pouted. 'You like?' she asked.

'You need tennis balls,' replied Journee. 'How rude!' Chime laughed.

'Miss Awesome,' said Memory. 'Why are you wearing a mask, dear!'

'You know why I'm wearing a mask!' Journee replied.

'You'll get used to the smell,' she laughed.

Journee studied Memory's perfectly smooth white face, which had the appearance of an animated balloon.

'Whoops, forgot my torch!' said Journee, turning back.

'Such a Fuss Bucket problem!' replied Chime, and in an instant was glowing from head to toe like a fluorescent light. It was as if someone had flicked a switch. Memory was also bright white.

'OMG, that is so cool!' said Journee.

'Bless you, dear,' Memory replied. 'It's just a silly old Underer trick, but it does come in handy.'

How wonderful to have your very own personal torch. Two of them actually! The only light was from the Underers themselves, who resembled walking torches. Memory held her hand out, guiding Journee down the first few steps. Chime led the way, springing down the stairs like a supercharged slinky.

'One, two, three, four, five!' she hollered. 'She always counts stairs,' said Memory. 'Has done it ever since she was a small white thing.'

Memory hummed a happy tune while stacking leftover cereal boxes and other household rubbish from above. She adjusted the antenna on her head. 'How silly of me! I forgot to ask whether your family had any deliveries recently? A pizza maybe-?'

'-Or a piano!' Panic added.

'Actually, now that you mention it, we have!'

she said. 'A pizza *and* a piano.'

Mother and daughter giggled. Journee's face turned from confusion to fascination.

'That was you?' she shrieked. 'That was *you!*'

'We have all sorts of fun.' Memory winked.

101 steps later they reached the cool, dark beginnings of Shadow Edge.

'Oh, Journee,' said Betty. 'I wanted to thank you.'

'Thank me?' she said, skidding to a stop.

'For this,' said Betty holding a tray with a crispy roast chicken and golden potatoes. It smelt absolutely delicious.

Journee was speechless.

'What a lovely surprise it was,' said Betty. 'When did you learn to *cook* like this?'

'I…um…school…I guess.'

Betty sniffed the food and smiled. 'Well, I've got to say I'm most impressed. Tonight we shall have a feast, a FEAST, and *Miles* can do the dishes.'

'Huh?' said the boy, rolling off the couch for effect. 'Sucks! Why me?'

'Because the chef never has to clean up!' said

Betty.

'Thanks, Mum,' Journee sang, and skipped towards her bedroom. Once she got there she thought how very clever and thoughtful her new friends were.

Journee had learnt many things about Underers in the last few days. She learnt they were very creative beings and over the years had thought of many ways to protect themselves. Like the ingenious trick they used to trap and kill Poppers without getting popped themselves.

It was a trick Journee forced herself to remember.

She also learnt the reason they didn't set off house alarms, like a human or a household pet might when an alarm is set. This is because the infrared light can't detect their see-through bodies. Underers can move about houses however they please.

'But we still have to be careful,' Memory had told her. 'When we pick up an object, like a jar of peanut butter, or a television remote. The infrared of the alarm might not detect our bodies, but the alarm will sound when it sees the movement of the things we might pick up. Which is why we always make orange cake in the pantry.'

'The pantry? Why?' Journee had asked. 'Because there is no alarm sensor in there, dear.' 'Am I really the first Fuss Bucket you've met?'

Journee asked.

'Of course you are,' said Memory. 'We had no reason to meet one before.'

'But Fuss Buckets must have seen you. What about the people who lived in our house before us? Someone must have seen you.'

'We are a discreet and peaceful people,' Memory said, giving a friendly wink. 'Apart from when we beat up burglars.'

'Hmm,' Journee mused, not altogether happy that she had everything sorted in her mind. She knew as much as anyone that life wasn't always tidy, that there were some things even teachers couldn't answer. But as she sat 101 steps from her home, she longed to know more about these bizarre new friends she had found by chance. Where did they come from? Other questions, hundreds of them, sat on the tip of her tongue.

'Memory, can I ask you something?' she asked.

'Sure, just don't ask me to sing.'

'What…are you?'

'I am *me*,' Memory replied.

'You're not human, but you can talk. You don't have to go to work, or school, you don't even wear clothes. You live under our house and drink mud!'

'Lovely it is, too, dear, you know that.' 'But…but…how did you *get* here?' 'Down the stairs, just like you,' she said, giggling.

Journee folded her arms, a fake stern look on her face.

'If you must know,' said Memory, 'we escaped.' 'From where?' Journee replied.

'One day Panic and I crawled beneath the cracks in the floor of your house. We snuck down past your basement and arrived here, where you are standing, Shadow Edge.'

'But how?'

'Well, this is some time ago, dear, but I do remember someone leaving the Underer 600's door wide open, and lucky for us, because back then there neither Panic nor I had the strength to open it. Even now we can't open it because it is too high to reach for little squirts like us. We would need a ladder! So anyway, the Underer 600's door was open and Panic and I saw the outside for the first time. In a split second Panic and I chose to escape!'

'Wait, wait, wait!' said Journee, shifting towards Memory. 'The Underer 600? Isn't that the-'

'-Alarm in your house, dear, yes it is.'

Journee's thoughts flashed back to the night she forced open the door of the Underer 600 and found hundreds of adorable little beings dancing and frolicking.

Memory continued. 'You must understand, it became too dangerous for us to live in there. So one day, when we were both brave enough, we decided to do something very scary: we left.'

'Because you could no longer fit in the nest?' 'Yes, that's right. And when we found this new home, it felt so much like our old one, only bigger.' 'You know, my dad says he has never seen an alarm like it.'

'Have you ever seen anything like us?' Journee smiled.

CHAPTER 8

Journee found a seat in the corner of Cave 6164 and held her nose tightly. There was still that nasty stench, as if someone was cooking an old pair of trainers.

'Who's for some Popper casserole?' beamed Memory. 'Please don't tell your mum I borrowed her pot.'

Panic was reading a book called *101 Ways To Beat Up Burglars*.

'Are there really that many ways?' Journee asked.

'Of course!' said Panic. 'You can trip 'em, punch 'em, squash 'em, sit on 'em, jump on 'em, kick 'em, torture 'em, squirt 'em and eat 'em!'

'*Eat* them?'

'Affirmative!' Panic replied. 'They would taste robbery.'

'You mean lov-er-ly?' Journee teased.

'Rob-be-ry. Instead of lov-er-ly,' replied Panic. 'It is a joke, a humorous anecdote, or remark intended to provoke laughter.'

'You need to meet my brother,' said Journee, giggling.

'Why ever would I want to do that?' Panic asked.

Journee studied Panic's face closely. *How old is he*, she wondered. Unlike humans, none of these strange underground beings appeared to have any wrinkles. Memory and Panic looked no older than Chime. They were just slightly taller.

Meanwhile, Chime grinned and handed over a small, shiny piece of metal. It was gold in colour, the size of a fat pen with a sharp end.

'My present! To you!' said Chime. 'I've had it since I was a small white thing.'

'Thank you,' Journee replied. 'But what is it?'
'A medal from World War VI,' replied Chime. 'Are you sure? There have only been two world wars.'

'I found it beside the Loopoopaloopoo,' Chime replied, ignoring such details. 'Now it's yours.'

Journee held the glowing medal in her hand. It was still warm from being in Chime's pocket. She put it in her own pocket, buttoning it tightly. 'I'll keep it forever,' she said.

'That's because friendship is forever!' Chime replied.

As Journee sat with the Underers, she felt a cool breeze coming through the cracks in the walls of the cave. Not for the first time, she wondered what lurked in the deep darkness behind the walls.

She was now familiar with Burglar's Alley, and the Loopoopaloopoo, but those steps, where did they lead to? Were there more caves? Were there more Underers? What might she find?

Memory was napping now, so Journee stood very quietly and snuck to the entrance of the cave. She peered in both directions. Chains rattled in the distance. She squirmed as a big gloop of water from the stony roof above dripped down the back of her shirt.

'BOO!' came a voice. 'AARRGH!' screamed

Journee.

It was Chime. Journee slapped the Underer playfully, and barely had time to regain her breath before she felt her arm being tugged towards the path behind the cave.

It was pitch black, so much so that Journee would have seen more if she shut her eyes completely. She crept behind Chime, feeling the sides of the slippery walls with her fingertips.

'Want to see some car-wazy?' Chime asked and stopped abruptly. 'Don't tell Mum and Dad.'

And the small white dot was off.

'Wait, Chime!' Journee said, wiping the sweat from her forehead. 'What *kind* of car-wazy?'

'Forgot Ma Legs!' came the reply. 'Forgot your *what*?'

There wasn't a lot of room behind the cave, just enough for a tight alleyway. And rubbish, lots of it. Journee held her nose and coughed violently. 'Chime,' she asked. 'Are you sure we're allowed around here?'

'Not long now, Miss Awesome!'

'But are we *allowed* out here?' Journee asked.

'Yes and no,' giggled Chime.

'Yes or no?' 'Mostly no.'

And she was off, again. Journee really wished she'd stop doing that. It would be nice if the Underer realised Fuss Buckets weren't walking torches like their white blob friends.

She continued to feel her way through the tiny space, treading ever so carefully on slime and goo and disgusting brown water. Just a step or two away was a slither of light, which became wider the closer Journee got to it. Soon she didn't have to crouch at all because the alleyway was wide enough to spread your arms and breathe.

Which is exactly the spot where the small Underer appeared to be juggling something. Were they ropes? No, not ropes. They were…surely not… Chime was juggling snakes.

Real.

Live.

Snakes.

'You took your time,' said Chime, as the snakes hissed and scrambled mid-air.

Journee backed off immediately. 'What…what

are they?' Journee asked.

'Forgot Ma Legs!' said Chime, as if she was a circus clown juggling oranges. Suddenly the snakes slipped from the Underer's hands and onto the ground. They slithered all around, taunting her. Three slithering serpents testing the nerves of a child.

'You are crazy!' Journee said. '*I* am crazy! What am we doing here?'

'Oh, I see,' said Chime. 'You'd rather be in maths with Miss Carboni?'

Journee grabbed a nearby stick, but Forgot Ma Legs were far too skillful to be worried about a Fuss Bucket with a make-believe sword. They slithered in and out of the cracks in the rocks around her.

Seconds later the Underer was off again, slipping between hidden passages.

Twenty paces away was a hole, but not just any type of hole. This huge crater was the type of hole only mountaineers or cave climbers would be crazy enough to venture down. It was a big, black pit to nowhere, about five metres across and incredibly deep, with seemingly no bottom.

Journee peered down into the darkness.

'Where does it go?' she asked.

'Who knows?' Chime replied. 'It's called Last Ditch Ledge.' And she picked up a tiny stone. She dropped it into the hole and waited. Nothing…then, perhaps ten seconds later, a barely audible *tink* sound.

As the smallest Underer miraculously sprung across in one leap to the other side of the huge hole, Journee heard something else. The sound came from behind, and it was more terrifying and dreadful and frightening than anything she had ever heard. She turned quickly.

Something scrunched. And crunched. Whatever it was made its way along the narrow path she'd walked along just seconds before. There was another sound, a hissing this time. And it was very, *very* close.

'Memory? Panic?' Journee asked. 'Is that you?'

Journee stole a look at Chime on the other side of the hole. Her aerial had turned a nasty shade of red. It buzzed and fizzed wildly.

Suddenly Journee really needed to pee.

'RUN!' cried Chime. 'It's the Eye-Shiner! Miss Awesome, run, please!'

Have you ever seen those TV shows where some know-it-all expert in tight brown shorts tells you how to behave if you see a dangerous animal? Sometimes these experts offer other useless advice like, if a gigantic beast is heading towards you and is clearly going to eat you in one bite, stay perfectly still! Or punch the man-eating shark in the nose.

Journee discovered this rule did not apply to a very hungry crocodile. This was the sort of beast you would only find in a museum, dead, or at the very least, stuffed. Its armour was more suited to a gladiator. As it grunted and heaved, saliva dripped from its spiky jaws.

Journee had never seen such a terrifying beast. If there was a more disgusting animal on earth she couldn't think of it. One thing was for certain. This was no time to twiddle your thumbs!

The crocodile lurched forward, thumping its clawed feet along the edge of the hole. Journee froze. She soon realised there was only one option. The scaly creature now blocked the pathway.

This would be a very good time to say that most Fuss Buckets, and even Underers for that matter, can outrun a crocodile. But it won't come as a surprise that a crocodile will always out-surprise you, for as long as two-legged beings have walked the earth, these creatures have unexpectedly popped up out of nowhere and munched and crunched their victims without so much as a, 'Hello, how do you do?'

Journee scrambled to her feet as the animal thundered towards her. She tiptoed around the dreaded hole. The Eye-Shiner was gaining. This was his territory now. *Snap! Snap!* The crocodile's jaws were now so close to Journee she could hear their echo.

Suddenly something grabbed her by the arm and whooshed her away.

Journee screamed so loud it echoed through the underground like a firecracker. She wriggled and punched and yelled, before looking behind to see the creature that had snatched her. It had a glowing white face and an aerial.

———

Journee and Chime sat silently in Cave 6164. Panic paced about like someone awaiting very bad news. He double-checked that every lock on the front door was tightened. Then he stood on a rock, peering through a tiny space near the cave's roof, a space no bigger than a small bird.

'All safe, dear?' Memory asked.

'For now,' grumbled Panic. 'But that doesn't mean he's not coming back.'

When Panic walked towards Chime, she offered him her chair, which Journee noticed looked very familiar. But Panic chose to stand instead. He folded his arms and said nothing. His face was yellowy grey, and his aerial fizzed and popped like sparklers on a birthday cake.

'Before you say anything, Dad,' said Chime, sitting up as straight as possible. 'Journee had never seen Forgot Ma Legs before, and I know Last Ditch Ledge is out of bounds but-'

'-You know the rules,' said Panic.

'But it's so *boring* down here, there's just smelly burglars and-'

'-Chime, please,' said Memory. 'We know you love adventure, but rules are rules.'

'Is that our chair?' Journee asked. 'We're borrowing it,' said Panic.

'I need it for my homework,' Journee said. 'It's

the perfect height for our computer.'

'Told you they'd miss it!' said Panic. 'We should borrow things they don't notice, like socks, or teaspoons, or sunglasses. I'll make some mud tea; who would like a cup? I'll do that now.'

Panic grabbed Chime by the arm and placed her back into the stolen seat.

'Thank you, Panic,' said Memory. 'Now, Chime, as I was saying. We are well aware you are keen to show Miss Awesome every part of Shadow Edge, especially things like Forgot Ma Legs, but you've also got to realise that when you do we worry for your safety. And why do you think that is?'

'Flash?'

'Yes, Flash.'

Chime folded her arms. Her antenna wobbled slightly, before drooping like a dead flower. Journee sat a little closer to the smallest Underer.

'What's Flash?' Journee asked. 'You keep talking about Flash.'

'Well,' said Memory, and paused for so long Journee thought she had forgotten what she was going to say. 'Our little family…used to be four.'

'Four?' said Journee. 'What happened?' 'We used to have a little one, smaller than

Chime,' said Memory. 'He was named Flash. We lost him when he was just a little white dot.'

'You *lost* him?' Journee asked.

'He used to wear a little superhero cape. Spider- Man, was that the one, Chime?'

'Yip, Spider-Man,' replied the smallest Underer. 'He wore it everywhere,' said Memory. 'I'm sure the boy's parents upstairs used to wonder where all of their capes went, but little Flash could not keep his hands off them. Then one afternoon we were coming back from 88 Cabbage Tree Avenue. It was a lovely afternoon; we had made orange cake and played the piano all day. Then when we were walking down the 101 steps, Flash ran into a tiny cave to hide. He loved to hide. That was the last time we saw him. Then Panic saw the Eye-Shiner swimming down the Loopoopaloopoo.'

'There was a cape floating behind him,' said Panic.

The cave was silent.

CHAPTER 9

The next morning at school Journee's shadow loomed over Miss Carboni as she placed the letter gently on her teacher's desk.

'Let me guess!' said Miss Carboni, her eyes glued to 'Stupid Cat Fails' on her computer. 'Very important doctor's appointment?'

Journee tried to swallow, but there was a tennis ball in her throat. 'Yes, Miss Carboni.' 'You don't look very sick to me.'

'It's…my breathing.' Journee replied, feeling utterly lousy muttering every word. 'This doctor, he's a specialist.'

'You'll miss English,' muttered Miss Carboni. 'Which no doubt is the reason you're doing it.'

If she was honest, there was something far more pressing on her mind than missing English. What Journee really wanted to know was the answer to a ridiculous, but important question.

How on *earth* did a crocodile end up beneath her house?

Today the cave didn't feel so homely. It was colder than usual. The walls were wetter, smellier. When Journee touched them, damp clay dripped onto the palms of her hands. Memory nibbled on freshly baked brownies, but Journee sensed there was pain behind her smile.

Chime was silent, Panic abnormally so.

'What's wrong?' Journee asked. 'Something is wrong.'

'It's October,' said Memory. 'Which means the floods are coming.'

'When it rains plenty in Fuss Bucket Land,' Panic added. 'Water gushes down here and we have monumental danger, even more danger than normal.'

'What sort of danger?' Journee asked. 'More Eye-Shiner danger,' Panic replied. 'The…*crocodile*?'

'Yes, the crocodile,' said Chime.

The Underers were silent.

'Do you remember the night we met, dear?' Memory asked. 'How we said we needed your help?'

The three Underers looked to Journee. Chime managed a kooky smile.

Suddenly it dawned on her.

'Wait!' said Journee. 'No way…you want me to catch a *crocodile*?'

'Eye-Shiner!' Panic said. 'Eliminate Eye-Shiner.

Destroy! Extinguish! Do away with!'

Journee's half-eaten cookie lodged in her throat.

'You want me to *kill* a crocodile?' 'Eye-Shiner!' Panic corrected her.

'The rains cause floods,' Memory said. 'Floods bring Eye-Shiners.'

'I don't have a lot of experience *killing* crocodiles!' said Journee.

'Bad winter brings Eye-Shiner,' said Panic. 'We could be next lunch.'

'Get Panic to do it!' Journee cried. 'He's strong, he beats up burglars!'

'Fuss Buckets are easy, Eye-Shiners are not,' Memory replied. 'You must help us, Miss Awesome. We wouldn't ask you unless we believed you could do it.'

Journee was speechless.

Panic moved in closer. 'We are in dangerous,' he said.

'No, no, no! Definitely not!' Journee replied, and stood abruptly. 'I have to go. I've got homework to do.'

———

Journee woke after a deep sleep. She felt ready. Yes! This was the day she would ask her dad if she could get her phone back. She knew very well there were still two days of her week-long punishment to go, but hadn't she done well not to complain?

Not once had she asked for it back. And anyway, she felt a newfound confidence since arriving in her new home. She had come eye to eye with a crocodile, dodged guano, and stood over Last Ditch Ledge without falling in. Asking her dad to cut short her phone curfew would surely be a piece of cake!

So Journee put on her new socks, brushed

down her school uniform and tied her hair into a bun. Her stomach was fizzy, and her legs felt like jelly, but as she walked down the hallway to the kitchen where she felt tall, strong, *ready*. She knew exactly where her dad would be, at the table feeding Ringo and Moses crusts from his toast.

Only he wasn't.

Journee heard a door slam and watched her dad stumble out of the bathroom, unshaven, his shirt untucked, and make a beeline for his car keys by the front door. He didn't even acknowledge the dogs, despite them jumping up on him for their morning pat.

'Bye,' Bill Blake mumbled. 'Off to the office.

Be back late, big job today.'

'Bye, honey!' Betty Blake replied, not looking up from her newspaper.

But Mr Blake wasn't going to work. Journee discovered this when she handed a note to Miss Carboni and ran home at 2 p.m., and saw him sitting in Fraser's Cafe with his head in his hands. He was crying.

Journee felt her knees buckle and her head spin.

She felt for her dad, but she also worried deeply about what all of this meant. Just as she was beginning to enjoy Millwater, and Bonnie-Kate, and her Underer family, her life was about to be tipped on its head.

Again.

———————

The walk home from school was long and tiresome. When Journee finally reached Cabbage Tree Avenue, she felt as if her shoes were filled with rocks. She dumped her bags on the floor and untied her shoelaces. She stopped.

Oh man, there was homework to be done, and dishes to be washed, but she couldn't bear to think about her problems above ground, so she quickly re-tied her shoes and opened the secret door. Ninety-one steps later she saw a familiar face standing on the muddy floor of Shadow Edge.

It was Chime, who was holding a bucket, her aerial crackling and fizzing.

'Miss Awesome!' she cried. 'Just in time!' 'Just in time for what?' Journee asked. 'Why do you look so happy?'

'For the first time, EVER, Mum has said that *I* can feed the burglars!'

'Oh, wow, that's great…I guess?' Journee replied.

But as usual, there was no time for chit-chat, which suited Journee just fine. She felt herself being dragged towards familiar tunnels and alleyways, sucking in the cool, damp air.

As the two set off they heard the familiar clatter of chains. Soon, a criminal caught a glimpse of Journee. 'WOT CHOO DOIN' BRINGING DAT PORK CHOP BACK 4?'

'DON'T COME ANY CLOSER ELSE WE'LL EAT YOU UP LIKE CHIPS IN SAUCE!' said another. Chime snuck up to the hideous thieves, her face all but touching theirs.

'Do you want me to set the Eye-Shiner on you?' Chime teased.

'PLEASE! WE DON'T WANT TO DIED LIKE DEAD PEEPS.'

'Well, you'd better be nice to us, then!' replied Chime.

'ANYFINK FOR YOU, ROYAL HI-NUSS.

HULLO, FATTY PORK CHOP!'

'You guys are mean,' said Journee.

'NOT AS MEAN AS HIM!' criminal number one said pointing to his neighbor. 'HE KIDNAPPED A GRANNY!'

'IT WAS EASY PEASY!' said criminal number two. 'SHE COULDN'T SEE OR HEAR! I GOT HER!'

'You kidnapped a poor old granny?' Journee asked. 'How old was she?'

'NINETY_ONE, PORK CHOP.'

'THAT'S NUFFINK,' said another burglar pointing to the man with no teeth. 'HE'S GOT BODIES IN THE FREEZER AT HIS HOUSE. HE WENT INTO A BANK AND BORROWED SOME MONEY.'

'You borrowed some money?' Journee asked. 'THEN ONE DAY I WAZ DRIVIN DOWN

THE ROAD AND A CAR FOLLOWED ME. IT HAD BRIGHT FLASHING BLUE LIGHTS. AND THE MAN WEARING A HAT PUT ME IN JAY- ALL!'

'How many years were you in jail?'

'LEMME SEE. TEN YEARS FOR PUTTING MY FRIEND IN THE FREEZER. FOURTEEN FOR BORROWING SOME MOOLAH FROM THE BANK. THAT'S THREE YEARS ALTOGETHER!'

'Wow!' said Journee. 'Your math's is amazing!'

'Look out, Miss Awesome!' Chime yelled. 'Who wants a rotten apple?'

'ME! ME! GIVE IT!' said a criminal, and the smallest Underer crept very carefully towards the thief, who opened his mouth wide, showing off his yellow, worn teeth.

'*Nicely!*' said Chime pushing the rotten apple towards the man's mouth. He scoffed the disgusting piece of fruit in one bite. The Underer once more reached into her stinky bucket. 'Who's for a chicken bone?' she asked.

'DAT'S MINE!' yelled another criminal. 'YOU PROMISED LAST TIME, YOU DID, YOU PROMISED!'

Chime handed across the bloody chicken carcass. 'Nicely!' she said, and the burglar did as he was told, trying to use his chained-up arms to attack the vile meal.

Journee was beginning to feel decidedly ill. 'Chime?' she said. 'That's…what you're feeding them…is that all from our rubbish bin upstairs?'

'Sure is!' she replied. 'Who wants a fish head?' 'YAAAAAAAAAAH!' And the recipient chowed into the fish's face, eyes and all.

Journee stepped back, balancing on a nearby rock. 'But that's-'

'Disgusting?' Chime asked.

'Yes! Disgusting! My dogs wouldn't even eat it!'

'They *didn't*,' Chime replied. 'That's why we're feeding it to these sticky-fingered Fuss Buckets!' For her final act, Chime dived into the bucket and pulled out the most repulsive thing of all. 'Now, because you've all been so polite,' she announced. 'We're going to leave you all with some ROTTEN EGGS TO SUCK ON! How does that sound?'

'EGG! EGG! EGG!' cried the criminals.

'Chime,' Journee whispered. 'Do you think we might be able to leave now, I think I'm going to be sick.'

'Ha! Miss Awesome, you'll get used to it. Next time *you* can feed them!'

'I think I'll stick to my brownies, thank you very much.'

And with that the girls walked off, the clatter of chains rattling behind them.

'Can I ask something?' said Journee. 'Anything, Miss Awesome.'

'Those burglars, there are four of them. Are you telling me they all tried to rob our house?'

Chime nodded casually.

'But how long have they been there?' 'Long time,' said Chime.

'How long?'

'Ha, years! I'm sick of the smell of them.' 'Years? But don't people in Millwater wonder where they are?'

'Most probably, but these Fuss Buckets have no right to steal. We take our job of guarding 88 Cabbage Tree Avenue very seriously.'

Journee stopped and looked into the Underer's small black dot eyes. 'Can I ask another question?'

'So many *questions*!' Chime replied. 'The Eye-

Shiner,' said Journee.

Chime aerial on her head cracked and popped. 'Don't talk about him! I hate him, HATE HIM, HATE HIIIIIIM!'

'But how did it *get* down here?' Journee asked. 'Stupid thing escaped from animal house and…and…swam here in Fuss Bucket foo-foo!' 'Animal house?' Journee replied, and it finally clicked. 'The *zoo*?' she continued. 'Millwater *Zoo*? The Eye-Shiner escaped from the zoo?'

'Animal house!' said Chime.

'But…that can't be right,' said Journee. 'It sounds *impossible*.'

But Chime had already left, slithering her way through the tunnels of Shadow Edge. 'Stupid dumb Eye-Shiner,' she mumbled.

By the time Journee reached Cave 6164, she hoped like crazy Panic had forgotten about his ridiculous request from the day before. Besides, how exactly was a ten-year-old child supposed to extinguish a man-eating crocodile? Strangle it? Poison it? Call it names?

As per the rules, Journee took her shoes off

and within seconds mud and slime soaked her socks.

'What a wonderful day we've all had!' said Memory, sipping her mud tea. 'We played piano and made orange cake. We are so grateful for your home.'

Journee was a smart girl. She knew what was coming, but before she could reply, Panic jumped in. He said, 'Now, since you've been so generous as to exterminate the Eye-Shiner we would like to-'

'Panic, I'm so sorry,' Journee replied. 'But I've been thinking about this whole crocodile thing and I'm not really that sure-'

'-We would like to return the favour!' Panic continued, winking. 'It is Underer way. You do good, we return good. We have noticed your brother gives you cramp in backside.'

Journee looked to Chime, confused.

'He's a pain in the butt!' said Chime.

Journee giggled. 'Yes!' she said. 'Miles is a pain in the butt.'

Panic continued. 'Is there anything, for egg-sample we could do to ruin your brother's life? Just a little, nothing too serious. Maybe something like our famous pizza delivery trick? Or the expensive piano?'

Journee sprung from her seat as if it were an electric fence. Suddenly the thought of the Eye- Shiner and the dangers of Shadow Edge were gone. She had a wonderfully masterful plan to annoy her most annoying brother.

Which she whispered into Memory's ear.

Was there anything worse than sharing breakfast with a brother who just talked and talked and talked? Today was one of those days.

'Got a riddle,' said Miles, prodding Journee with his index finger. 'There's this man and he walks out into the rain. He doesn't have a raincoat. Or an umbrella. He is wearing shorts and a T-shirt. His clothes get soaked but his hair doesn't. Why not?'

Journee felt for the envelope in her pocket.

'Why didn't the man get wet?' Miles repeated.

'Huh?' said Journee.

'Why didn't the man get wet?' 'I don't care, Miles.'

'Cos…he was bald! That's why he didn't get wet!' said Miles. 'Because he had no hair!'

'I know what bald means,' said Journee.

'You know,' said Miles. 'If you actually laughed

more you'd have more than ZERO friends.'

As if Journee needed reminding. Now she watched her father sit at the breakfast bar and read the newspaper in his dressing gown. 'Dad?' she asked. 'Is everything alright?'

Mr Blake wiped the sleep-dust from his red eyes. He looked broken. He also smelt like something you might find in Shadow Edge.

'You lost your job, didn't you, Dad?' Journee asked.

'What are you talking about?' he snapped. 'I saw you in Fraser's today. You weren't wearing your uniform.'

Mr Blake ruffled his hair vigorously for at least thirty seconds, as if he didn't want to hear or see anything that resembled real life. He looked right through Journee.

'I work with imbeciles! I get no respect. Sergeant Cat Vomit said I wasn't allowed to work at the station anymore. So I said, good, well I quit! And he said, you're fired! And I said, I quit! Then I emptied my strawberry milkshake over his head.' He sniggered at his own joke, but Journee didn't laugh.

She collected the plates and sighed.

'Please don't tell your mother,' said Mr Blake. 'She couldn't bear to move again.'

'But what will you do for money?' Journee asked. 'Mum's waterproof karaoke business isn't exactly working. Or NightBuilders.com.'

'No!' said Mr Blake, and this time it was a hearty, honest laugh. 'They're not really, are they?' Journee waited. 'So?' she asked.

'So what?' her father replied. 'What will you do?'

'That's my problem,' Mr Blake whispered. 'Please. Don't say anything.'

Aren't worries a funny thing? They always manage to push themselves ahead of all the goodness inside your head. Worries are impatient and greedy. They get all the attention, like the class bully. If only we could pop them like a balloon and give our good thoughts the best seats in the house.

Journee had two bully-sized worries. The first was the Eye-Shiner. Didn't the Underers wonder where this beast *came* from? How long had it lived beneath innocent people in Cabbage Tree Avenue?

Imagine if Journee's neighbours knew that a terrifying beast, longer than the car in your driveway, with a voracious appetite for anything that walked on two legs, had ended up roaming a sewer beneath where a young girl slept. As if that worry wasn't big enough, Journee also couldn't help but think of the awful prospect of having to move houses again.

But for now, at least, there was dinner to look forward to, which began in the lounge where Miles was picking his nose in front of the TV.

Journee bit her nails in the kitchen behind him.

She watched the front door like a starving lion watching an antelope. Seconds later there was a polite knock.

'Door!' Journee yelled, her heart thumping erratically as she slunk towards the bathroom. 'I'm on the toilet.'

'Miles, get the door!' came another voice. 'I'm busy!' replied Miles.

Mr Blake raised his voice. 'Get. The. Door.'

Miles kicked the cushions across the room and stomped towards the door. Journee waited at the end of the hallway, able to see everything. As usual the door stuck. Miles pulled and pulled and eventually fell over like someone at the end of a tug-of-war rope.

Smiling back at him, holding fresh flowers and a bottle of wine was his teacher, Miss Moyle!

Journee squealed silently. The back door slammed.

'If that's someone selling a pizza or a piano they'll get a slipper in the mouth,' said Mr Blake, who arrived at the door to find his son lying down. His face was the colour of a tomato. Miles quickly tucked his shirt in.

'Can I help you?' Mr Blake said to the guest. 'I'm Miss Moyle.' The attractive lady smiled.

'Miles' teacher.'

Mr Blake frowned, then grinned. 'What's the trouble now?'

'Quite the opposite,' said Miss Moyle. 'I'm…here for dinner.'

'Must be some mistake.' Mr Blake turned around, about to yell to his wife, before remembering she was out.

'Betty kindly invited me,' said Miss Moyle. 'Where shall I put the flowers?'

Twenty minutes later the World's Most Awkward Dinner took place. It wasn't the food, despite it being as tasty as toasted toenails. It wasn't even the dogs, though Moses licked Miss Moyle's knees continuously. It's what happened next that Journee wished she had caught on video, and it all began when she asked a very simple question.

'Miss Moyle,' said Journee. 'Are you enjoying your dinner?'

'Yes, Journee,' the teacher replied, sawing her meat into pieces. 'It's…very well cooked.'

'Mind if I smoke?' Mr Blake asked. 'Please don't,' replied Miss Moyle.

And Mr Blake did as he was told. And then his eyes lit up like glow sticks.

It was very rare for Mr Blake to tell jokes. Other dads entertained their children by doing leg farts, or gargling silly songs, but not Mr Blake. His was a very serious face, which he'd always worn every day to his very serious job. Which surprised Journee, because she'd once read that many policemen were extra funny, because it made their extra serious jobs not so serious. But not Mr Blake. Many things were far funnier than he.

'Miss Moyle?' said Mr Blake, stubbing out his cigarette.

'Yes, Mr Blake.' Miss Moyle smiled. 'That's your real name?' he asked. 'Miss

Moyle?'

'Yes, Mr Blake,' replied Miss Moyle.

Miles buried his face in his hands.

Mr Blake continued. 'As in, do you like *Miss Moyle*?' he said.

'I've heard that joke many times, Mr Blake,' said Miss Moyle.

'Do you like *Miss Moyle*!' Mr Blake repeated, smiling from ear to ear.

'I don't get it,' Journee said.

'Do you like Miss Moyle?' hollered Mr Blake.' I got new teeth. Do you like Miss Moyle!'

'Oh!' said Journee. 'Do you like Miss Moyle!' 'So? Do you like Miss Moyle?' Mr Blake asked. 'Yes, I do like your Smoyle!' said Journee.

'Do you like Miss Moyle, Miss Moyle?'

Right now, the only part of Miles' body visible above the table was his face, which switched from pink to red like one of those mirror balls at the school disco.

Miss Moyle tried to chew her meat, but she might as well have been chewing on a bumper boat. When she thought no one was watching (Miles was) she hid the gristly pulp underneath her one piece of limp lettuce.

She caught Miles staring. 'Maybe after dinner you can show me your room?' she said.

'He'll have to pick up his *Power Rangers* undies first!' said Journee.

And Miss Moyle laughed loudly. Mr Blake laughed louder.

But Miles wasn't laughing. He wanted to die. He had never seen Miss Moyle away from the classroom. He knew as well as anyone teachers aren't real outside school. They simply don't exist outside of the hall and playground. They don't go to the mall. They don't drive cars and they certainly don't sit in your house, on your chairs, and watch you eat the worst food on earth. Then Miles had the most horrendous thought.

The most horrendous thought.

Tell me she's not going to sit on our toilet!

'Where is your toilet, please?' Miss Moyle asked.

Miles couldn't help it. It was all too much. The thought of his teacher putting her bare bum on his toilet seat and scrunching his toilet paper! He spewed his food right up. Burnt chops and Brussels sprouts landed on the table in one mashed clump.

Even if someone wanted to wipe away the mess, they wouldn't have been able to, because two uninvited guests spotted a wonderful opportunity.

In one fell swoop Ringo pounced onto the table and wolfed down Miles' leftovers. Poor Moses felt left out, so he followed and bit Ringo's tail to get a piece of spare meat.

Mr Blake went to whack his dogs with his slipper, but he was never a good shot and missed completely, instead belting Miss Moyle right across the nose.

A red welt appeared almost instantly. As she rose to her feet, her skirt got caught on a nail under the table and seconds later there she stood in the Blakes' lounge in her bright pink knickers.

Ringo loved this game and decided that a skirt would be the perfect thing to bury. He began to run towards the yard. But Moses loved another game, tug-of-war, and soon the floral skirt lay in tatters on the lounge floor.

The front door opened and in walked Betty.

Miles looked at Journee. Journee looked at her father. Her father looked at Miss Moyle, who covered her legs with the tablecloth.

'Anyone for dessert?' he asked.

CHAPTER 10

The next afternoon Journee bounced into Cave 6164 and landed directly on Memory's lap.

'It was *so* funny!' she said. 'You should have seen his face!'

Memory smiled a devilish smile. 'We try not to overuse that little trick.'

Journee took leftover homemade chocolate brownies from her school bag and passed one to the Underer.' You know what I like about you, Memory?' she said, munching merrily. 'You're always so happy.'

'That's because life is a blessing, dear,' Memory replied.

'But you live in a sewer! There are Poppers that can pop you. Eye-Shiners could eat you!'

'Awful things happen to Fuss Buckets, too,' said Memory.

Journee did not look convinced, so Memory continued. 'If I had nothing but Panic and Chime I'd be as happy as a kitten with a ball.'

For the first time Journee had a chance to really study Memory's face. Up close it resembled a giant, dim light bulb. But it was free of dust; it was soft and warm and peaceful.

Memory smiled and her antenna buzzed a little more than normal. She was now inches from the girl's face. 'And now I have you.'

'Stop delay, Fuss Bucket!' said Panic. 'You owe us. Pain in backside with brother gone. We did good, now you do good! Eye-Shiner will eat us for suppa! Chew us like cake. And you will neva see none of us eva again.'

'Hey!' exclaimed Journee. 'OMG! I've just worked out something. Your *names*. There is a *Memory* button on the old alarm upstairs. And a *Panic* button. And one that says *Chime*. And they're your *names*.'

Panic strode across to Journee, his stone-cold face inches from hers. She could smell his fear. Then the Underer pointed to the cliff, where the Eye-Shiner's teeth shone like tiny swords.

'No more talk,' said Panic. 'Kill the beast.'

Suddenly Journee needed to pee *really* badly.

There was a rat in Room 5. An oversized, greasy, stomach-churning rat that could probably swallow an entire child during Brain Break and still have room for dessert. The class screamed as the overfed beast fell from the ceiling. It landed on all fours before venturing into the art cupboard. Miss Carboni scrambled onto her desk like it was a life raft.

'Erma gard!' she screeched. 'Somebody get a broom! Or a stick! Kill it! *Kill* it!'

The rest of the children were either very excited, or very scared. Journee was neither. She was calm.

She stood and walked towards the art cupboard. She had seen a wonderful trick 101 steps below.

Miss Carboni was on her knees now, on top of her desk. When she spotted Journee she pointed to the open door. 'It's there!' she yelled. 'In the corner. Underneath the paints!'

'Okay,' Journee replied, calmly.

The rest of the children, mouths agape, whispered and scorned her as Journee entered the cupboard. The cupboard itself was no bigger than a small bathroom, cluttered with powder paint, washable paint and almost every other kind of paint. It really was a small space.

The rat couldn't have been more than a few feet away.

'It's a rat!' said Miss Carboni. 'In there! I saw it!

It was going to eat my leg!'

Journee rolled her eyes and sat on the floor. Her heart was beating fast, but she wasn't scared. A memory came back of something she had seen at Shadow Edge. Yes, she thought, that will be perfect! She opened the door ever so slightly.

'I need peanut butter and a spoon,' she said to Miss Carboni.

'What are you talking about?' said Miss Carboni. 'Just get the rat!'

'I will,' said Journee. 'But I need peanut butter and a spoon.'

'I've got a spoon!' said Bonnie-Kate, rummaging feverishly in her lunch box.

'I've got a peanut-butter sandwich,' said another boy, who passed both through the tiny gap in the door. 'Good luck,' he said. 'You're…very brave.'

Journee looked back at the boy. He wasn't joking.

'Thanks,' she replied, blushing red.

Journee unpacked the sandwich and scraped the peanut butter off with Bonnie-Kate's spoon. Then she smeared peanut butter over the handle end of the spoon and balanced it on the bench in front of her.

There was a big square bucket full of scrap paper. She emptied it and placed the bucket beneath the balancing spoon with the peanut butter.

She waited. The lunchtime bell rang. There was a loud knock on the art-cupboard door.

'Are you dead, Fatty Vampire?' yelled a classmate.

'Did you marry the rat or something! Ha! Ha!' said another.

When the noise died down, Journee opened the door again, just a touch.

'Miss Carboni,' she whispered. 'I've got a plan. Don't open the door. I think I will have the rat by the end of lunchtime.'

'Whatever!' said a boy. 'Like a girl could catch a rat!'

There was a large black curtain in the art cupboard where other supplies were kept. It was just big enough for a ten-year-old girl to stand behind.

And it was the perfect hiding place. There was even a box she could sit on. Journee opened the curtains, found a seat, and closed the gap.

The classroom was quiet. Suddenly something stirred behind the powder paints. The sound was followed by a feverish scratching noise. And then it happened. The rat scuttled up the side of the cupboard, stopping abruptly beside the spoon.

The animal sniffed the air. With no thought whatsoever it ran out to get the peanut butter and in an instant fell off the end of the spoon into the bucket! Journee parted the curtains and grabbed some tracing paper.

She covered the bucket and poked a hole in the top.

Twenty minutes later the rest of the class arrived. Journee held a bucket on her desk. One by one the children looked inside the small hole in the tracing paper. And one by one they peered at Journee as if she were some type of superhero.

Bonnie-Kate pulled up a chair beside her.

'Where did you learn to *do* that?' she asked. 'My new friends,' Journee replied. 'You can meet them one day.'

'I would love that,' Bonnie-Kate replied.

'I can't wait to show you,' she said, and was about to tell her absolutely everything, until Miss Carboni arrived. She strode in with the principal, Mr Snark, who was joined by two other very serious-looking teachers. They saluted Journee, army style. Mr Snark stood between the two men and adjusted his tie.

'As you well know,' boomed Mr Snark. 'We take health and safety very seriously in this school.' He pointed his forefinger directly at Journee. 'You saved the day, Miss…?'

'Blake,' said Journee. 'Journee Blake.'

'Do you know something?' said Journee. 'If you call them Poppers they're not nearly as scary.'

'What aren't?' said Mr Snark.

'Rats!'

'How true. From now on these disgusting creatures shall be known as Poppers, as named by Journee…'

'…Blake!'

'As named by Journee Blake, the great Popper Catcher of Room 5!'

The entire class burst into applause. Bonnie-Kate hugged her.

Nothing in Journee's life could beat this moment.

Nothing.

CHAPTER 11

Journee despised walking home in the rain. She despised it even more than her brother, more than spiders, even more than running. The way those drops of iciness dripped down your neck and onto your warm skin. The way your socks squelched and slipped inside your shoes, not to mention the way your clothes stuck to your body like a shower curtain.

The point is, such a walk would normally put Journee in a very stinky mood. But not today. Not on the day she'd caught a child-eating rat with her bare hands and become Class Hero.

Mr Blake was in the driveway when the children arrived home. He stumbled out of the car in his dressing gown, carrying a bag of soda bottles and a newspaper. Soon he joined them on the porch, shaking the wet from his umbrella.

'Hi, Dad?' Journee said. 'Busy Friday?' 'Very,' replied Mr Blake.

'I got a certificate for bravery.' Journee beamed.

'Cos she caught a teeny-weeny mouse,' said Miles.

'It was a rat,' said Journee. 'And it was bigger than your brain.'

Bill Blake reopened his umbrella. 'Forgot the stupid mail,' he sighed, walking to the mailbox at the driveway's entrance. Miles unlocked the front door and it swung open with a creak. He was about to switch the alarm to the OFF position, but something wasn't right. The machine on the wall began to beep and screech randomly. It shook violently.

'What the...?' said Miles, desperately trying to yank the alarm's arm. 'I can't turn it off!'

He tried again. Same result. Seconds later Journee saw something which shocked her to the core. It was as if she had been punched in the chest by a professional boxer. She tried to keep her balance, but her knees buckled and she fell to the floor.

In front of her lay Memory. She was breathing loudly like a wounded animal.

Journee's gaze turned to the kitchen. The secret door was slightly ajar. Memory's eyes, normally jet black, switched to a dull yellow.

'What the heck is that thing?' Miles yelled.

Journee was too shocked to think. 'Miles, help me pick her up. She's sick. She might die.'

'Are you kidding? I'm not touching it! Dad!'

Miles backed towards the front door and glared at his sister as if she were bat-wing crazy.

'Please!' Journee said. 'I promise I will tell you later what this is all about.'

Outside, Mr Blake stood at the letterbox and screwed up one envelope after the other.

Journee knelt beside Memory and stoked her forehead. 'Memory, it's me, Journee. Can you hear me?' The Underer lay limp and groaned.

'You are seriously weird,' said Miles. 'Oh, wait, is this one of those TV shows with a hidden camera? It is! And is this a fake alien? I get it, we're being filmed!' He spun around in a circle and waved at imaginary cameras. 'Hi, everyone! You thought you got us! Nice try!'

Journee put her ear to Memory's mouth. She was alive, at least she was alive, but her breath was short and shallow. In the movies when someone collapsed people gave mouth-to-mouth resuscitation. But this wasn't a person. This was a… Miles was right. What was this?

'Grab her legs, I'll take her arms.' Journee pointed to the trap door. 'We'll put her in there.'

'Why is it making that noise?' Miles asked. 'Just do it!' said Journee.

'Ew, it feels squishy.'

Journee lifted and carried the Underer across the lounge, her eyes clogged with tears.

'It was the Mazemaker! The Mazemaker did it!' The voice belonged to Chime and came from behind the kitchen cupboard. Miles' tarantula Webster slunk across the coffee table.

Journee looked at Webster, then at Memory, then at the alarm.

'The Mazemaker,' Chime repeated. 'It was the Mazemaker!'

Journee stamped her foot loudly. 'Miles!' she yelled. 'Put that disgusting thing back in its cage! And distract Dad!'

Journee slammed the secret door behind her.

CHAPTER 12

At the top of the stairs Journee found Panic and Chime holding each other like two frightened children. With no idea how to handle an Underer, Journee picked Memory up and passed her awkwardly to Panic, who cradled her in his arms.

'We need to get her away from the infra-red!' said Chime. She led the way down 101 steps, past bats, past drainpipes and sewers. This time Journee didn't count the steps. She looked into Memory's eyes, but they had faded to a sickly yellow colour, like her father's hair had faded from smoking too many cigarettes. 'Miss Awesome?' she mumbled. 'The Mazemaker…it was the Mazemaker.'

'It's okay, Memory,' Journee said, tears

forming. 'We will get you home. Just relax.'

Mr Blake marched into the kitchen with the mail from the box. 'What was all the noise about?' he asked, noticing the rug was strewn across the floor. He stood with his hands on his hips. 'Where is she?'

Miles searched for something to say, but what? How was a boy, whose sister had taken some sort of alien through a wall in the kitchen, supposed to answer such a question?

'I said, where is she?' said Mr Blake. 'She…went to the shop,' Miles stuttered. 'To buy a…' He looked around the kitchen. '…fridge.' 'Fridge? Really? Where is she?'

'She…went for a jog,' Miles said.

'Now I know you're lying. Anyway, it's raining.'

Miles looked around for something, anything to get him out of this mess. 'She's…in the garage,' he said. 'Doing a project.'

Memory lay on a stony bed. She was so still, her skin no longer off-white in colour, but light blue, like the sea. Panic brought over mud tea and touched Memory's antenna with his. But Memory's antenna had burned black.

Chime laid his head on her chest. 'It's my fault,' she said. 'It's all my fault.'

'It's not!' said Journee.

'Memory always said not to go into your room because of the sticky door. So I didn't. But I forgot. I was in your room and the door closed behind me. I didn't think. Then the wee-woo-wee-woo…' Chime stopped and sniffed.

'But I don't understand,' Journee said. 'Couldn't someone have let you out?'

'Chime was taking food from your pantry to 6164, because the floods are coming and we need extra,' said Chime. 'When the Mazemaker walked in front of the sensor the wee-woo-wee-woo went off. I screamed and screamed. I was trapped. Your door stuck. I heard Memory on the other side. She finally opened it, but then collapsed. The wee-woo-wee-woo was so painful. I tried to drag Memory through the trap door in the kitchen away from danger.'

'But you didn't collapse, like Memory?' said Journee.

Chime began to cry. 'My batteries are newer.'

'It's not your fault,' said Journee.

'Panic found us at the top of the stairs and carried us towards the secret door,' said Chime. 'But Memory was already… Why didn't you tell us you had a Mazemaker?'

Journee had been listening so carefully to Chime she failed to notice what was happening to Memory. She was shrinking before their very eyes. This beautiful creature was getting smaller by the second. Deflating like a balloon.

'What's happening?' Journee asked.

'She is leaving us,' said Panic. 'Soon she will be the size of Popper. Then gone.' He placed his hand on her head. 'Memory always said, life precious. Not the body we remember, but spirit.'

Memory's body continued to diminish. Seconds later, a puff of blue smoke filled the cave, making it impossible to see anyone or anything.

Two sounds followed. One was the sound of Chime sobbing. The other was the sound of two dogs barking from above. There was no choice now.

Journee quickly left Cave 6164 and ran up the steps towards home, where Mr Blake waited.

He slammed the kitchen bench with his fist.

'Where have you been?' Journee said, 'In the…' 'Garage!' said Miles. 'Doing a project!' He winked at his sister. 'For school?'

'Yeah, just a dumb project.' Journee put her filthy hands behind her back.

'Have you been crying?' Mr Blake asked.

'Got some dirt in my eye,' Journee replied, and swiftly took off towards her room. But she stopped beside the old alarm. Who had left the door open? More to the point, how did anyone manage to open the ancient machine's door in the first place?

Journee peered inside. She saw the nest.

All of the tiny white people were dead.

As usual, the bedroom door stuck, but for once it was a blessing. If only she had her phone. It was still two days until she was allowed to have it back. If she had it now she knew exactly what she would do – text Bonnie-Kate and tell her everything. What was the point in holding onto this stupid secret anymore? It was impossible to hold everything inside her. She felt as if she would burst. The last thing Journee needed was her brother's annoying face in hers. But it didn't last long. Miles eventually managed to pull the door free.

He walked in with Webster, smiling.

'Get that thing out of here!' Journee said. 'What was that white thing lying on the floor?'

he demanded. 'It looked like an alien. Does it live in the cupboard?'

'How did Webster escape?' asked Journee. 'He didn't,' said Miles. 'I let him out.' '*Why?*

Miles shrugged. Journee threw a sock at him. 'You are so mean!' she said. 'Why would you do that?'

'Why do you think? Cos you invited Miss Moyle to dinner.'

'I did not!' Journee replied.

'Don't lie,' said Miles. 'Mum said she never asked any stupid teacher to come over. And Dad doesn't even know what school we go to. So it must have been you.'

'It wasn't me,' said Journee. 'I promise.' 'Liar.'

'It wasn't me, Miles.' 'Pants on fire.'

Journee buried her head in a book, which happened to be upside down. Miles stomped across the bedroom and flipped it the right way up. 'If it wasn't you,' he said, 'then who was it?'

Journee leant over and turned the stereo up, just a little louder than normally.

'Shut the door,' she said.

Journee told Miles everything. How she had met a white blob family. How she had grown to love them. How they lived underground, and how a sewer crocodile stalked them as the Blake family lay in bed 101 steps above.

Miles' entire fist sat in his mouth. 'Where are these people!' he said. 'I got to meet them!'

'You can't,' Journee replied. 'You'll tell your idiot friends. You'll tell Mum and Dad.'

Miles flicked his shoes off and flung them across the room. Instant stink.

'Fine,' he said. 'Don't show me. I'll tell Mum and Dad anyway.'

Was there anything more dangerous than a dumb brother who had nothing to lose?

Journee bit what was left of her thumbnail. She worried. She worried first about Chime. Then she worried that her wonderful secret would be snatched away. All because of a dumb spider and its even dumber owner.

Journee leapt from her bed and took Miles into the kitchen. Betty was fast asleep in front of the TV. Mr Blake was nowhere to be seen. Meanwhile, Ringo had a cap in his mouth. It was Chime's. Perhaps it had fallen off when she attempted to escape when that stupid spider belonging to a stupid brother set off a stupid alarm.

'Drop it, stupid!' Journee whispered to Ringo and grabbed hold of the cap. But the dog yanked it from side to side. 'Ringo!' she repeated. 'I said drop it!'

Ringo growled. What a great game this was!

Miles pulled Journee's hoodie. 'I wanna see the white blobs,' he said. 'Forget the stupid hat!'

'I can't,' said Journee, tugging forcefully at the cap. 'It's…I have to give it to someone.'

'Who?' demanded Miles.

'One of the white blobs,' said Journee.

She glared into Ringo's eyes. Her world was caving in again. Soon everything would fall apart. The Blakes would move. There would be a new school. And a new house, with someone else's germs, their arguments, and, well you know the rest.

Miles pushed his sister aside and held the dog by the snout. Then he blew on the dog's face. 'Ffffft!'

Ringo shook his head and whimpered. The cap hit the floor.

Miles shrugged his shoulders. 'Old trick,' he said.

Journee pushed all of her weight against the secret door and eventually fell through to the other side. She shone her torch down the damp, slippery steps. She plodded down with a dry throat and a heavy heart.

Miles pushed Journee aside and whooped and hollered like a child let loose in a theme park.

Journee sighed. Once upon a time she had been the excited one, falling into the dark unknown, unaware of the wonder that existed just a few steps below.

But those feelings belonged to Miles now. Journee cleared her throat and wiped her eyes.

This would be the final goodbye. She wanted to make it last, to savour every second, to remember every single thing about her best friend. She wanted to be grown up about it all, to be there for Panic and

Chime

The children reached the flat ground of Shadow Edge in a slow haze. Poppers hid in the towering rocks around her. Bats dropped guano on her shoulder. She didn't flinch.

'Argh!' screamed the boy. 'Some things are landing on me!'

'Guano,' said Journee, completely uninterested. 'What's g-?' Miles yelled.

'Bat poo,' said Journee, peering up.

Miles glanced to the ceiling of the cave.

Thousands of eeny white eyes glared back at him. He knew all about bats, how they could eat six hundred bugs in an hour, how some people called them flying mice, and how they slept upside down. And here he was standing below hundreds of them. Miles could have stayed there all day, but his sister didn't. She was already gone.

Miles placed a bat skeleton in his pocket and lumbered through the damp alleyways of Shadow Edge. He soon caught up to Journee, who was in no mood for light conversation.

'What's that noise?' Miles puffed. 'It's like a

beep, beep, beep.'

'They're talking,' Journee replied. 'Who's talking?'

'The Underers. That's how they talk. Now shush and keep moving.'

The questions kept coming. So many questions! What colour is their poo? What do they eat? Is that a sewer? Where does their pee go? Where are the shops? Who owns the cap again? *What colour is their poo?*

Journee stopped outside 6164, her heartbeat pounding in her ears.

'Is that where they live?' asked Miles. 'The white things?'

'Yes,' Journee replied. 'Now stop asking questions!'

'Okay, sorry.' Miles bit his lip, then seconds later continued, 'Is there a toilet down here because I really need to-'

'Miles!'

Boom! BOOM! Booooo-OOOOOOM!

Journee looked ahead. A tower of purplish steam exploded from Cave 6164. Bright yellow sparks, like lightning, fired from the cave's windows into nearby rocks, causing them to crumble like sand.

And then, silence.

CHAPTER 13

Journee scrambled to the top of the steps without counting a single one. Miles followed closely behind, bounding into the kitchen like a toddler on Christmas morning.

'What was all that smoke?' Miles coughed. 'I couldn't see a thing!'

But Journee couldn't answer Miles' question, because even though she was no stranger to the world below, she had absolutely no idea what had caused the rainbow-coloured explosion.

Not that it mattered anyway. Journee's best friend was clearly now nothing more than a memory. She dusted off her coat and moped towards her bedroom. The dogs scuttled along behind her, their paws sounding like a hundred mice as they ran across the wooden floor.

'What are you doing?' Miles asked. 'Aren't we going back?'

'No,' said Journee.

'But don't you want to see if the white things are okay?'

'No,' said Journee.'

'Journee!' said Miles, and held onto the back of his sister's T-shirt.

'Leave me alone,' she said.

'You have to go back, you said they were your friends!'

'I'm never going back,' Journee replied.

Later that night, when Journee tried to shut her eyes the tears pushed them open. Even Miles couldn't fall asleep, which was especially strange given the same boy once fell asleep face down on a floor filled with Lego. He even once fell asleep on the toilet. And in a shopping trolley at the supermarket. In his school uniform. While dribble dripped down his chin.

But this time she wanted her brother awake. She missed his voice.

Journee switched on her bedside lamp and opened the top drawer next to her bed. Hidden beneath her school notices was a poem Memory had written one day while she was at school. The poem was just one sentence, but a sentence Journee found herself reading every morning and night. It said, *You may be small, but you are powerful. Always remember that.*

Journee stared at the ceiling and remembered the first time those strange white things had stood at the foot of her bed. Memory hardly spoke that night. She never was the bossy one.

Very late at night, or it could have been very early in the morning, Journee's eyelids became heavy and she was taken away. Soon she felt like she was floating, on a sea, and the waves kept crashing into her eyes, stinging them, bringing new tears. Much like when you swim in the ocean and accidentally open your eyes in the sea water.

She turned her pillow over because it was too wet to sleep on, then she curled up like a cat in front of the fire and held her breath.

There's a saying that good things happen to good people, but in Journee's life every time something good happened, another thing twice as bad occurred.

She figured that's just how life was.

'You look like you've been crying, honey?' said Betty at the breakfast table.

'Just tired, Mum, that's all,' Journee replied, and she tried to swallow her food but all she really wanted to do was hide under the table, or beneath her bed covers.

She looked at Miles, who winked back. Journee felt as if she had rocks in her tummy. Terrible questions arrived in her head. What if the explosion of yellow and blue smoke caused something even worse to happen? What if Memory wasn't the only one who had died?

Mr Blake dinged his knife on his glass of milk. 'I wanted to share some exciting news,' he said, and every word that came out was like a tiny black cloud filled with sadness.

'Moving? *Again?* Miles asked. 'Why?'

Journee glanced at her mum and whispered. 'Did you know, did he…?'

'Of course, he told me, honey,' she replied. 'I knew all along, I'm not silly.'

Miles threw his hands into the air and both his

knife and fork did somersaults across the table, splattering egg across cups and plates. 'What is *happening?*' he asked.

Mr Blake frowned. 'Son,' he said, 'we're no different to every other family in Millwater, we need money to live.'

'But where are we going to go?' Journee asked. 'That's the exciting bit!' he replied. 'We're gonna get in the car and drive!' 'With no plan?' Journee asked.

'We don't need a *plan*, Journee!' said Mr Blake. 'Who needs a plan? That's half the problem with the world today. Everybody thinks they need a *plan*. This is an adventure!' he said, and rubbed his hands together.

The room went silent. Betty picked up Miles' knife and fork.

Journee was so puzzled as to what to do that she even patted the dogs. When she looked at the secret door, Mr Blake noticed a tear on her cheek.

'Now, now,' he said. 'Think of the fun we're going to have.'

If Journee Blake ever became famous, or if she was ever interviewed on TV by a man in a pin- striped suit, and if the man in the pin-striped suit ever asked her the secret to becoming popular, the answer would be very simple.

Catch a rat.

Because today was the best school day of Journee's life. Each and every child from Room 5, even the bullies who once called her Fatty Vampire, fought, *fought* to sit next to her.

These same bullies even gave her a new name – the Popper Catcher. The same bullies even cheered when she received a certificate in school assembly.

And as if that wasn't enough goodness for one day, Bonny-Kate also played her at checkers. Which all goes to prove, of course, what a funny old thing life is. One minute your sandcastle is being kicked over by the class bully, the next everything falls into place, piece by wonderful piece.

But the good feelings didn't last, not even till morning break. Every time Journee looked around the room at the smiling faces of her new friends she thought about Memory.

Why couldn't her classmates have been nice to her from the beginning?

CHAPTER 14

Journee decided if there was one good thing about what happened to Memory it was that she didn't have to lie anymore. There was nothing left to hide. Even Miles knew now, and it was only a matter of time before her mum and dad found out.

When she arrived home, Journee took Chime's cap from her bed and waited for Miles beside the secret door. He saw his sister's tears and tried his very best to not ask the thousands of questions which sat on the tip of his tongue.

'You said you were never going back?' he said, biting his lip.

Journee ignored him and opened the secret door. 'What did I say about stupid questions?' she asked and plodded down the steps. 'Don't ask me what I'm doing, okay, just *don't ask*. Because I don't know what I'm doing.'

Her throat was dry and her heart was heavy. Poppers hid in the towering rocks around her. She didn't flinch. Bats dropped guano on her shoulder.

She didn't care. She tiptoed along the path she knew so well, worrying greatly what she might find.

'Do they really drink mud, like you said?' asked Miles.

'*Did*, you mean?' replied Journee.

'*Did?*' Miles asked, his mind doing its best to think straight. 'Oh, I get it, because they're-'

'-Dead!' said Journee, and now her eyes were all fogged up again. 'And, yes, they really *did* drink mud because that's what you do when you live underground. We're not all the same you know. Not everyone is like you, some people are actually funny, and kind. And they were my friends, they weren't like you. They didn't scare people just for fun, or let their stupid Mazemakers out just to get *back* at somebody. And they *did* drink mud because if you live underground you drink anything you can find because life is hard down here. Have you ever had to *catch* a crocodile?'

Miles took a step back and studied Journee's face. In that split second he decided his sister wasn't like the other girls at school. She wasn't scared of anything. What other girl her age would come down here in the middle of the night and become friends with alien-like strangers? How did she all keep it all such a secret? How could she never have told anyone about the crocodile? How scared she must have been.

My sister's a bit of a legend! And he was even about to tell her, until something caught his attention, almost making his heart jump out of his chest.

'Journee, who is that?'

'Who is *what*?' she replied, and spun around to see a blur of white, blue and green bounding towards them. It was the unmistakable figure of Panic, who took Journee by the hand and was so excited he flung her straight into Cave 6164.

Journee fell to the ground with a thud. A few seconds later, though it could have been a whole hour, or even a day she was that dazed, she opened her eyes and saw her leg was cut.

She tried to stand, but she felt like a new-born calf, all wibbly and wobbly on her feet. She blinked and focused, then she remembered.

Panic stood in front of her, and she was about to wallop him for throwing her around like a rag doll, but just as she was winding up to punch him she turned around to find Memory lying on a boulder with a candle beside her.

She lay there as still as a tree, her antenna dull pink in colour, her face light blue.

Journee got down on her knees and pushed her hair back, placing Chime's cap on Memory's head. She then stroked the Underer's face, expecting her to be as cold as a river stone. To her surprise she was warm, like a laptop. She suddenly turned to Panic, who was nodding very slowly and very happily.

'We are very fortunate, Miss Awesome,' said Panic.

Journee cupped her hands over her mouth.

'The 6164 only took thirteen per cent of her capabilities,' said Panic. 'But the poor thing won't be blasting rainbow laser beams or going near a sensor for a while.'

'So she's…?'

'Alive, affirmative!' Panic replied, and he smiled like a baby in a bubble bath.

In his excitement Panic demanded a long set of high-fives. Sixty-eight of them to be exact. Underers never did things in halves.

'But, but, but, but, but, but, but, but, but, but,' said Journee.

'What, what, what, what, what, what, what, what?' Chime replied.

'But, but, but, but, but, but, but, but, but, but?'

'Got that part.'

'The explosion? I thought that the, the, the, the, the…'

Chime threw her arms around Journee from behind. 'That was just Panic. When Memory woke up he celebrated. Too much,' she said. 'He shot thousands of rainbow laser beams into the underground. One after the after! Too many after the other! Explosions!'

Journee felt the blood return to her head. She even managed a smile. Moments later Memory opened her eyes and held out her arm. 'Miss Awesome?' she whispered. 'You came back.'

Journee felt the tear fall down her cheek. 'I didn't go anywhere, Memory.'

During all of this Miles might as well have been watching a chicken ride a motorbike on the moon.

The boy felt as if his feet were giant boulders. Just as Journee had been when she first saw these strange beings, he was transfixed. He stared and stared, not so much as blinking.

'I need to touch one of these freaks. You guys are so weird-looking,' he sneered. 'Wait, is that my football? That's my football! You white blobs stole my football!'

Panic snatched the ball like a hen protecting her eggs. 'Finders keepers, losers weepers!'

'It's mine, stupid white blob thief!' Miles retorted.

Suddenly Memory sprung up and fired a gigantic rainbow laser beam from her belly, which only narrowly missed Miles. 'Go and eat sand, roof- sniffer!' she yelled.

Panic smiled at Memory. 'Her state is definitely improving,' he said.

As any child with good manners knows, it is

always polite to introduce new guests. In Journee's case, that guest was Miles, but brothers, as we also know, aren't exactly guests.

Besides, Miles was already well known to the Underers. Many times over the past few months they'd had the displeasure of moving his putrid socks so they could sleep on his bed. Or tiptoe around where he had missed the toilet and peed on the bathroom floor.

Despite this, Journee was a very polite girl and felt she should make a formal introduction.

'This is my annoying brother,' she said, and Panic and Chime nodded graciously.

Journee smiled so much it hurt. She watched as Memory sat peacefully, glowing like an angel. Her antenna fuzzed and whizzed, swaying from one side to the other like a blade of grass in the wind. She stretched her arms wide as Journee lunged towards her, hugging. Memory was soft and squishy, like a marshmallow.

There was a wonderful new smell too, like a freshly opened packet of bubble gum, all floury and sweet.

She was back. She was Memory.

It's one of life's oddities that just as we get something we want we create new problems. On the one hand, Journee couldn't have been happier.

Memory had been saved. On the other, she had news which sat on her tongue like steaming hot pie. It simply had to come out.

The cave was incredibly quiet, with none of the noises of a typical house. No hum of a fridge, or whirring of a dishwasher. Just the constant drip of brown water from above. Memory was fully awake now, her antenna buzzing bright green and blue. It was a miracle.

'Um, so, anyway…I…I have some news,' Journee said, finally.

'Oo!' said Panic. 'I like news, let me guess! You've figured out a way to trap Mazemakers for good! No, you've convinced everyone upstairs to make their own beds. I am sick of doing that job, and

I do hate an untidy room.'

'My news isn't good,' said Journee. 'It's…well, you won't be seeing me again.'

'Why ever not?' asked Memory.

'I know why,' said Panic. 'Her father is on fire.'

'He got fired,' Journee replied, correcting her small white friend. 'And now we have to move because he emptied an entire cup of strawberry milkshake on Sergeant Vomit's head and won't be allowed to work in Millwater again.'

Panic burst into laughter. In fact he laughed so hard his face seemed to heat up like a lamp. And just like a lamp, it changed colour, to yellow, pink and finally bright red.

'Fuss Buckets and their jokes,' Panic said. 'This is not a joke,' Journee said. 'Why would I

joke about something like this?'

'You are forbidden to leave until you zoop the

Eye-Shiner,' said Panic. 'We did good, you do good.' 'It's not *my* fault my stupid dad can't keep his stupid job!' Journee exclaimed.

Memory sat down and ate some dead flies she found on the rock. 'I knew this day would come,' she said. 'I have yet to meet a Fuss Bucket policeman who can handle the dangers of Millwater. We try our best to make life safe for everyone upstairs by zapping burglars, but it doesn't seem to make any difference. Millwater police are always on fire.'

'Fired,' Journee said, correcting Memory. 'We did good, you do good.'

'Panic, please, I can't catch a stupid crocodile. It's huge, and I'm small, like you.'

'You are capable of so much. Remember the Popper in your class?'

'Memory, that was luck. Anyway I didn't think of that. You showed me.'

'But you did it. When everyone else was running scared and standing on tables, you took the lead. You must have belief, but also courage. We would never have survived so long if we had neither.'

'But it's easy for you. Underers have superpowers.'

'And faults, just like Fuss Buckets,' said Memory.

'But you can do anything, I can't even make friends without them running away.'

'When I was a small white dot, about Chime's age, I was a frightened, timid mess. When we get older we get bolder.'

'But, Memory, look at me! I'm nothing compared to that Eye-Shiner. He'll eat me like chips and sauce, even Panic said so. If I could do it, I would. Even my dad couldn't wrestle the Eye-Shiner. Memory, why don't you do it? Blast the Eye-Shiner with your rainbow laser beam.

'I do not have the answer, Miss Awesome. I wish I did.'

'Does Panic?'

'He would have thought of it by now. Bless him, he is a hard worker but spends more time tuning his antenna or teasing Poppers. He can't think like I know you can. There is magic in that head of yours, Miss Awesome, magic which is dying to burst out.'

'But how do I find it?'

'Our very being reminds us of danger; we can spot it instantly, automatically. We have managed Poppers and Forgot Ma Legs. And most of the time we can detect Mazemakers and Sneakabouts. But this problem is too big, Miss Awesome.' 'But…I…how…'

'Remember, you are small but powerful.' And when Memory turned the aerial on her head, Journee felt an excited buzz run all the way from her feet to her head.

CHAPTER 15

1.25 a.m.

Miles was off discovering Shadow Edge, but Journee barely noticed. Perhaps a caring sister would have warned her brother of sea snakes and crocodiles and deathly drops in an unpredictable, at times terrifying, world, a world where any young boy, or child for that matter, could perish in any number of ways, including getting eaten, stung or thrown about like a small teddy bear by reckless criminals at Burglar's Alley.

Yes, a good sister would have told him such information. But Miles always stole the couch, and that was something Journee never forgot.

Suddenly a body could be seen awkwardly splashing ankle-deep through the Loopoopaloopoo. It was Miles. Ten seconds later he stood in front of 6164, puffed and speechless.

'A crocodile!' he said, catching his breath. 'A big, giant crocodile! He…it…or she. Wait, it could have been a he? Or maybe it was a she?' The boy appeared confused. 'How can you tell the difference between a boy crocodile and a girl alligat-'

Journee shook Miles by the collar. 'What happened?'

'It…it…it took the small white thing!' Miles said.

Journee looked about the cave and saw only two Underers. She looked to her brother. 'Chime!?' Where is Chime! Miles! Trust you!'

Journee shoved past her brother, but her shouting was no match for the echoing howl of two dogs.

Journee's worst fears came true when she turned around to find Ringo and Moses. Behind them was her father.

And crawling through the river, just metres

away, a very familiar-looking reptile was searching for fresh meat.

You'd think crocodiles wouldn't like running upstairs. They have low bodies, like lizards, and are fine running on the banks of a river, but if given the choice would probably prefer to take the elevator. If only they could reach the buttons.

But this Eye-Shiner was not your average crocodile. Such a ruthless beast sits alongside other hideous creatures like Great White Sharks, box jellyfish and science teachers called Phil.

14, 15, 16 steps.

Journee played leader and bounded up the stairs quicker than anyone.

'Thanks for shutting the secret door, Miles!' she yelled.

'I did shut it!' her brother replied.

'So the dogs just opened it with their clever fingers! Or maybe your little spider friend opened it with his hairy butt!'

'Shut up, Journee!' 'You shut up, Miles!'

'Everybody be quiet!' yelled Mr Blake, fighting for breath.

34, 35, 36.

The Eye-Shiner's clacking jaws echoed through the cave. At least ten steps ahead of Miles and her father, Journee stopped briefly. The crocodile was gaining. Miles and Ringo, as clueless as ever, treated the deadly animal as if he were a toy.

Mr Blake tripped on step number 29 and his shoe came loose. He wiggled it loose and seconds later, SNAP! The Eye-Shiner spat it out and continued his chase.

59, 60, 61.

Journee watched her father stumble ahead. He heaved and spluttered, but he wasn't as young as he used to be and it showed. 'Miss Blake!' her father wailed. 'If we make it out of this alive you have a lot of explaining to do!

78, 79, 80.

While it was true Eye-Shiners enjoyed the taste of Underers, real live Fuss Buckets were a far more attractive option. Underers were little more than a pleasant snack, an entree or an appetiser. Any Eye-Shiner could devour an entire family in one sitting. It's very much like you and I enjoying a bowl of potato chips before dinner.

But eating real live people is a challenge, any crocodile will tell you that. For a start there are bones to deal with, and sometimes clothes can be a pain to chew, but what a tasty prize!

99, 100, 101…

The Eye-Shiner stomped and thrashed his way towards his victims. Mr Blake was in real trouble now; he was running so slowly it was as if he had rocks in his shoes. The Eye-Shiner was quite the opposite and had a real target in Mr Blake's butt.

CRUNCH! CRUUUUNCH!

'ARRRRRGH!' screamed Mr Blake. The Eye-Shiner had ripped a gigantic hole in his trousers.

Suddenly he found a little more energy and bounded up the stairs. He even found the strength to pick up a rock and throw it at the Eye-Shiner. 'Leave me alone, you stupid beast!'

With just a few steps left, Miles pounced into the kitchen. Journee guided her father through the secret door next, just ahead of the Eye-Shiner who showed off his razor sharp teeth and thrashed his head from side to side. Journee had a split second to react.

Once inside, she slammed the door shut right onto the Eye- Shiner's snout. Without so much as a whimper, it slithered down the stairs into the darkness.

Journee staggered into the lounge. 'Everything is ruined,' she said. 'Everything.'

Betty was fast asleep, but the rest of the family, including the two dogs, found safety in the lounge. Mr Blake was sweating, but not because he was tired. The expression on his face was one Journee had never seen. He wasn't angry. He was scared, staring at the secret door as if at any minute anything could come through it.

'Those terrifying white *things*, with the see-through skin,' her father said. 'Where did they come from? How did they get here! How did you find them?'

Journee made a decision, quickly. Before her dad could interrupt any further, she was going to repeat the story she'd told Miles, leaving nothing out. She sat tall on the sofa, her words strong and clear. 'They live underground, but they also live here.'

'Live *where*?' asked Mr Blake.

Journee opened her arms wide. 'Here!' she said. 'In this house.'

At times Mr Blake seemed to have trouble keeping up. His expression turned from surprise, to disgust, to wonder. 'I'll have to arrest them, you know that?'

'What for?' 'Ah…trespassing!'

'They were here before us.'

Mr Blake covered his mouth with his thick-set hands. He fell onto the seat and sighed heavily. There was pure fear in his eyes.

Journee continued. She said that the 'terrifying white things,' as her father named them were born from the old alarm on the wall.

Bill Blake sprung up like a startled bird. 'The Underer 600? Oldest house alarm ever made. Piece of rubbish, but possibly worth a lot of money to the right collector. Anyway, carry on.'

Journee told her dad how the Underers spent their days at the Blakes' house playing piano and making orange cake. How Mazemakers and Eye-Shiners were their enemies. And most importantly, how they'd made every single mess that Journee had been blamed for.

Mr Blake tried to make sense of Journee's

story. 'But Miles let his spider out, wasn't that bad? If he hadn't, that white thing wouldn't…'

'Memory?' Journee corrected him.

'Memory,' he said. 'Wouldn't have nearly died.'

Closing her eyes didn't stop the tears. They ran down Journee's cheeks, dripping onto her knees. She hugged herself tightly.

'This Memory white thing?' Mr Blake said. 'She's a friend of yours?'

'Yes,' said Journee. 'She's like a mum to me.' Betty woke. 'Where am I?' she said suddenly.

'What did I miss?'

'It might take a while to explain,' said Mr Blake and poured a cup of tea for his wife.

CHAPTER 16

The smallest Underer was not dead. The small white blob had even managed to sneak into the Blake household without so much as waking a dog or a spider. She now stood alongside her friend as she fell in and out of a restless slumber. Less than a minute later Chime got bored so she tickled Journee's feet. She wanted to scream like a school class on a roller coaster.

'You're…alive!' Journee whispered. 'But…but how? Miles said the Eye-Shiner chased you. I thought you had been taken.'

Chime jumped under the covers, leaving little room for Journee.

'I went to check on Fuss Bucket Miles,' said Chime. 'Suddenly the Eye-Shiner lunged out of the water, but I was too quick. I had to hide in a cave for seventeen minutes exactly. I was not happy.'

'Wow, first Memory and now you. Talk about lucky!'

'Are you really leaving Millwater?' asked Chime.

Journee nodded. 'I don't want to,' she said.

Chime stood on the end of the bed with her arms folded. 'In the vastly wide and varied history of Shadow Edge we have never experienced floods the likes of which we are about to witness. A low front is approaching Millwater from the south west which is likely to bring heavy rains and devastating loss to the city below. Such conditions will favour a sewer crocodile. Ignoring such warnings will likely bring more death and unhappiness. The future is in your hams.'

'You memorised that whole thing with your photographic memory,' said Journee.

'Maybe.'

'Memory and Panic sent you here to say that.'
'Maybe.'

'Did they?' Journee asked. 'Yes,' said Chime.

'And it's hands, not hams.'

The next morning Mr Blake ran into the lounge carrying two bulging suitcases, the dogs trying to attack his slippers as he walked. He began shovelling clothes, sleeping bags and pillows into the bags.

'Dad, please, no!' said Journee.

'Journee, please, yes!' he replied. 'Those *things*. We're leaving! Tomorrow!'

Journee hugged herself tightly. Mr Blake moved towards her and patted his daughter on the shoulder. 'Now come on,' he said. 'There's no need to be like that. Why worry? Those things, they're not even *people*.'

'They're family,' said Journee.

'*We* are your family. Those things, whatever they are, they have no place here. Not to mention the crocodile that lives with them.' He tried to pull whatever hair was left out of his head. 'This a nightmare. First my job, now this. We've got to leave!'

'Do I still have to go to school?' 'Absolutely, you still need an education!'

Everyone knows how hard school can be, but today was especially awful for Journee Elizabeth Blake.

Everything was annoying. Miss Carboni was annoying. Seb Grommit was annoying. English was annoying. Maths was annoying. The word annoying was annoying.

Journee knew why. Because one planet-sized pimple of a problem sat right at the front of her forehead. Eye Bleeping Shiner. The ants in her pants soon became too much and the idea in her head was bursting to come out. It was a risky-beyond-belief idea.

How risky beyond belief? Well, let's just say for her idea to be a success, for Journee Elizabeth Blake to save the ones she loved, she would have to kill an animal. Actually, two.

At lunchtime she left Millwater School for possibly the very last time.

Journee took off her water-filled shoes at the front doorstep of 88 Cabbage Tree Avenue. She threw her school bag in the lounge and ran to the kitchen.

And that, dear reader, is the exact moment Journee Blake had the most wonderful piece of luck.

The sort of luck only other people have, people who win lotteries, or marry a prince, or lose weight in two weeks by eating nothing but chocolate.

Journee's luck came from her mum, who was warming her hands with a cup of tea and staring at the rain as it hit the overgrown weeds in the backyard. 'Ringo's got one of the chickens in his mouth!' she screamed, completely aware of what she'd just seen, but having no idea what she should do next. 'Ringo, put it down! Put the chicken down, now!'

Mr Blake and Journee ran to the sliding door.

Ringo had indeed done as he was told, but the chicken was now an ex-chicken. It lay limp, dead on the ground in between the weeds.

'Naughty boy!' Betty added.

Journee Blake could not believe her luck.

In ten seconds flat she found her school bag and unlocked the back door. Into the thrashing rain she went. Oversized drops dripped down the back of her shirt, but she didn't think twice. Wading through long grass she found the dead chicken. Back at the window her parents were mouthing something but the rain and wind was so loud Journee never heard a word.

Then, somehow, despite every part of her body screaming 'Don't touch the dead chicken,' she reached down and touched the dead chicken. It was still warm, its body like a rag doll.

Journee looked away, put it into her bag, and ran inside.

Quite how Journee managed to whip past her father, who was trying to barricade the secret door, should be left to smarter people, but the girl with the dead chicken in her bag managed to do just that. It was a close call. When Mr Blake spotted Journee making a beeline for the door he knew exactly what she was up to. He even said a variety of words which are not appropriate for these pages, but Journee didn't flinch. Not for a second. Because nothing on this earth, or in this case below it, could be worse than moving house again. Especially when the ones she loved were about to be eaten 101 steps below.

If Journee had thought too much about what came next she would have locked herself in her bedroom forever. Because this idea was insane, mad-as-a-hatter, batty, bonkers. It was a completely gonzo idea and if it was going to work she would need to move fast.

And not think at all. But think a lot.

Yet not think at all.

Now we're overthinking it.

By the time Journee reached Step Number 101 she'd discovered two things.

Number one, that she'd forgotten to pee before she left the house. And number two, just how right Panic had been. Because the floods were here. An angry Loopoopaloopoo had awoken from its slumber, its waters bounding through the alleyways of Shadow Edge. A once calm, polluted stream transformed into an untamed and violent torrent.

But not too violent for the Eye-Shiner who roamed the river like a principal looking out for misbehaving children. For him, flood season was like Christmas. This was a gigantic lolly scramble and Memory, Panic and Chime were sweets.

Journee stood on the edge of the water. The Underers sat on their cave above the Loopoopaloopoo growing increasingly restless. Their antennas changed from green to yellow to red. They were obviously very stressed and worried.

The river was rising. Journee felt hopeless and helpless all at once.

'A disaster of epic proportions, Miss

Awesome!' Panic yelled. 'We have not seen such rain since Chime was a small white dot!'

Journee looked down to her feet where Forgot Ma Legs danced in the water. The presence of a crocodile made them seem more like pesky insects by comparison. She thwacked the snakes away with one swift swipe and the slippery beasts swam off.

The Eye-Shiner chowed them down as if they were cheesy pretzels. Journee had not planned for this moment. Her family were cornered. If they were to cross the river towards Journee they would become the Eye-Shiner's dinner. If they chose to go back towards their cave they would have to walk towards Last Ditch Ledge with its ginormous dangerous hole.

For Journee to reach them she would have to swim past a giant, hungry beast.

The Underers watched as the Eye-Shiner policed the current, his red eyes watching the white blobs above like a hawk. If he'd had lips the ghastly monster would have licked them.

Journee tightened the straps on her backpack and brushed the hair from her eyes. 'The river is rising,' she said. 'It's not too late; if we leave now we can run to our kitchen. We will be faster than the Eye- Shiner up the stairs. Now, jump! Swim to me!'

And that was the exact moment Journee Blake had the most awful piece of luck. The awful luck came when Journee looked into Panic's small black dot eyes. There was fear in those eyes, the type of fear which spelt certain death, if not something worse.

'Swim is not a thing we do,' Panic said. Journee's voice trembled. She turned to Memory, whose own antenna had switched to a

sickly yellow. 'You…can't *swim?*' she muttered.

'On account of our electronics getting wet!' said Memory.

'Water is biggerer danger than large sack of Sneakabouts, Mazemakers and Poppers,' said Panic.

'What happens if you get wet?' Journee yelled. 'Morbid Fuss Bucket!' Panic replied. 'We smoke, steam, bubble and melt. Happy?'

'But you live next to a river!' said Journee. 'Your cave is next to water!'

Panic threw his hands in the air. 'Swim is not a-' '-Thing we do, I know, Panic,' Journee replied.

Whoosh! A gigantic, filthy wave crashed

perilously close to the top of the cave rock and all of a sudden Journee's world started to cave in faster than ever. The shock of almost being touched by water caused all three Underers to huddle together.

'Meet me on the other side of Last Ditch Ledge,' said Journee. 'I've got a plan.'

'No!' said Panic. 'Last Ditch Ledge is lower than Cave 6164. We will smoke, steam-'

'Okay, Miss Awesome!' said Memory, and shot a scolding look at Panic, who nodded and smiled.

'Got your World War VI medal?' Chime asked.

'Right here,' Journee replied, waving the medal.

'You got this, Miss Awesome, the future is in your hams!'

'Hands!' cried Journee.

Journee watched as Panic led his family off the top of the cave. They soon became tiny specks of white.

Journee bent down and held two Forgot Ma Legs, which wriggled and squirmed and fought to get back into the water. Their long, leathery tongues flicked and wavered inches from her face. Ever so carefully, she threw the snakes as far downstream as she could, where the crocodile chased them like a Jack Russell chases a tennis ball.

Journee held her nose tightly and into the sludge she went. Thirty giant strides and she would reach the other side. Once on dry land, she scrambled up nearby rocks towards Last Ditch Ledge.

This was the perfect place for her deathly plan.

Exhausted, out of breath, and in so much trouble right now, Journee felt a tap on her shoulder. It was Chime, and she was patting the drenched school bag. 'What's in here?' she asked, sticking her face into the bag. 'It smells disgusting!' Suddenly her lovely white glow was covered in speckled brown feathers and blood. 'You brought dinner!' she exclaimed.

'Don't you dare eat that!' said Journee. 'And please, no more jokes or funny business, just be a good little white blob and do as you're told. And don't you dare run off. I don't really know what happens from here.'

The Underers waited on the opposite side of the gigantic hole to nowhere. If life were perfect, Journee would have told everyone everything was going to be just fine.

But the truth was, she had no idea if it was.

The hissing sound was back, and this time it was closer than ever. Suddenly, down the pathway came the Eye-Shiner. He flashed his teeth and glanced to the side, to get a better look at the ridiculously large main meal in front of him.

Memory and Chime both held on for dear life. Journee cursed herself. Surely it couldn't end like this. She tried to move, but her feet, her feet, were they glued to the ground?

Seconds later she picked up a long, wiry branch.

It was time. This was it.

Journee crept towards the hole behind the cave. The big, black pit to nowhere was five metres across and incredibly deep, with seemingly no bottom. She peered down into the darkness and very quietly unzipped her backpack. Out came a ball of string and the chicken, which was cold now, and limp, like a wet knitted toy, its glassy eyes still open.

Journee took a deep breath. She then grabbed the poor animal and tied its legs to one end of the long, flat tree branch. Then she slid the branch out towards the deep, dark hole, making sure it didn't tip by placing a big boulder on the other end.

Now the dead chicken hung upside down over the eerie, gloomy pit.

The Eye-Shiner sniffed the air, his scaly snout slowly moving from side to side. In the next few seconds, he would run for Panic and Chime with a plan to eat them up like chips in sauce. Well, that was the plan anyway, but Journee was so busy on 'chicken watch' she barely noticed the Eye-Shiner gallop like a rabbit directly towards her.

But the crocodile stopped abruptly beside the chicken on the tree branch. He sniffed the air again, but this time something dead and bloody attracted him.

And there it was, on the end of a branch just a few steps away.

Now don't forget, such animals work entirely on instinct. So it was, that with no thought whatsoever, the Eye-Shiner ran directly across the wavering tree branch towards what he thought was a delightful ready-to-eat freshly-killed meal.

Only when he got halfway across and within four paces of the dead chicken the boulder behind him rolled gently off to the side.

The cave was quiet. No one beeped.

For a split second the Eye-Shiner thought he might just make it back to land. Wrong.

In an instant he tipped off the end of the pole and fell down, down, down.

Ten seconds later there was a thud and a splat…and then nothing.

The Underers dropped to the ground with a tremendous thump, their antennas fizzing and zapping wildly. Chime clapped. Panic cheered. Rainbow laser beams pounded the rocky walls and multi-coloured glitter sprayed the crowd.

All three Underers danced and danced. Journee felt herself being lifted. She was thrown metres into the air, each time landing on a safety net of squishy hands. The first time she landed she screamed. The second time she laughed.

'It worked, Memory!' said Journee. 'My plan worked!'

'The Eye-Shiner is zooped!' said Panic. 'Gone

forever! Eliminated, exterminated, obliterated!'

'We did it for Flash, Memory,' cried Journee. 'That was for Flash!'

Memory wrapped her arms around Journee, who felt hot tears sliding down her cheeks. 'You are a risk-taker, Journee Blake,' said Memory. 'Now, I know Panic was very demanding of you, but you cared deeply. You wanted to help us so badly you dropped everything to make things better for us. You will never forget this, the moment you made so many lives better. I am so proud of you. I love you and always will.'

With Memory's warm embrace came that wonderfully familiar smell, like freshly opened bubble gum, floury and sweet.

'Same here,' replied Journee. 'Same here, *what*?' teased Memory.

'I love you too.' Journee smiled, and she thought back to the day she'd caught the oversized rat in Room 5. She remembered thinking nothing could ever beat that day.

She was happy to be wrong.

And to think the best part of her plan was still to come.

CHAPTER 17

11.58 p.m.

Journee's clothes were soaked and her leg was bleeding, yet somehow she found the strength to climb through the secret door. On the other side sat Mr Blake, who was watching TV and catching flies. Which is not to say he was literally whacking nasty little insects with a fly swat. 'Catching flies' is a figure of speech, meaning to sleep with your mouth so far open that to a fly it looks like an inviting cave. Such a fly did indeed actually fly into Mr Blake's mouth and that's when he woke up to the sound of voices, loud ones.

And steps, lots of them. He turned off his TV programme and tiptoed to the kitchen, but of course being a heavyset man he caused the wooden floorboards to creak like old bones.

Mr Blake put his ear up to the secret doorway.

'YOU CAN'T TREAT US LIKE DIS!,' said a brash, manly voice.

'HE SPEAKS DA TROOTH! WE'RE HOOMANS too!' said another.

'Keep your cake holes shut otherwise there will be trouble!'

Journee? That last voice was Journee's, Mr Blake was certain of it.

Suddenly the secret door burst open and five tattooed, hot-headed hooligans crashed into the kitchen all at once. It was a squeeze and half getting them all through such a tiny door, but Journee did a superb job. She yanked the chain which held the burglars together, forcing them to form a perfect line against the bench top, like school children in assembly.

What a motley bunch they were. Filthy, unshaven, toothless individuals. One eyed up the fruit bowl, while another flicked fresh mud from his shoes onto the spotless tiles. The smallest robber, a man no taller than Miles, wiped his nose and a trail of snot smeared across his hairy face. Mr Blake's mouth was wide open. He was flabbergasted.

Journee stood straight and tall. 'Dad,' she said. 'I'm sorry I'm late, but let me introduce some of the worst people in Millwater.' She turned to the burglars themselves. 'Gentlemen, meet my father – who also happens to be in the *police* force.'

A look of collective fear gathered on the robbers' faces.

'I DIDN'T DO IT, SIR! IT WAS HIM!' said one.

'I NEVER BROKE DA LAW IN MY HOLE LIFE!' cried the other.

Another attempted to run for the secret door, but fell over three other stinky men. 'THEY GOT THE WRONG GUY, DON'T PUNISH ME, I GOT GOLDFISH TO LOOK AFTER! THEY NEED AN EDUKATION!'

Journee strutted towards the kitchen door and passed the lead rope to her father.

'They're all yours.' She smiled.

Well, wouldn't you know it? When the morning newspaper arrived the next day, Bill Blake was the lead story. And here's what it said:

LOCAL POLICEMAN ARRESTS HORDE OF ROBBERS IN MULTIPLE RAID.

Bill Blake, a local policeman new to Millwater, became a hero overnight when he arrested four men responsible for numerous burglaries in the area.

Asked how he did it, Mr Blake was very humble. 'It was a team effort,' he said from the safety of his living room. 'We were fed a number of clues from the community and used those to work out where these bad people were hiding. It's been quite a journey.'

He slurped his coffee and sat back, a look of pride and happiness on his face. He turned to Journee, punching the air triumphantly.

'Sergeant Cat Vomit is going to love me! I'll get my own office! And a car park! And a birthday cake! And people will say, you're Bill Blake, criminal mastermind!'

'Ahem,' said a tiny voice.

'Journee, my dear!' he said, finally getting the hint, patting his daughter on the shoulder, knowing full well a hug was far too extreme. 'I don't know what to say,' he said. 'I feel so bad. I'm so sorry for he things I said. I was…I was…*angry*, and when adults are angry, we say and do things that are not right. Your mother and I are…both very proud of you.'

Journee's dad smiled a crooked smile. 'Now then,' he said, cutting out the newspaper article and securing it with a magnet to the fridge door.' What can I do for *you*?'

Without hesitation, Journee emptied her pockets. Out popped her World War VI medal and a crumpled piece of paper. She uncurled it and cleared her throat. 'My list,' she declared. '1. Move the dogs outside. 2. I get a *new* phone. 3. Keep the Underer 600.'

'What! Oh, no!' cried Mr Blake. 'No, no, no, look, let's buy a new alarm, one with Wi-Fi and all the mod cons and-'

'-KEEP IT!' said Journee.

Mr Blake backed away and nodded, trying his best not to appear unhappy.

'And number four,' Journee finished. 'I get my own room. I move in tonight.'

'Of course!' replied Mr Blake, his eyes once again focused on his picture on the fridge. 'You know, on second thoughts we should frame this.'

That night Journee moved everything she owned to the spare room where the dogs had once slept. She had a desk and her stereo, her headphones, her own lamp, and a drawer for her clothes. Her mum had even added a pull-out bed where Bonnie-Kate and Chime could stay.

Journee lay in her own room and smiled. A warm feeling came over her as she pulled the clean white sheets up to her chin. Her new family was safe and now that she had a new phone she could finally text Bonnie-Kate, to whom she wrote the following:

Journee - If you thought what I did to the rat was cool wait till you hear what I did today.

BK - Can't wait! You're too cool for school.

Journee - Seriously it's going to freak you out. You know those friends I said I wanted you to meet? They want to meet you too.

BK - Are they losers – or will I like them? Ha ha. LOL.

Journee - Let's just say you won't believe your eyes.

BK - Oooooo! Can't wait. Shall I dress up? #boys?

Journee - Just bring some old shoes and a jacket. BK - HUH?

Journee - Trust me. Goodnight, Bonnie-Kate. BK - Night, Journee. :)

Often in life the things we worry about never come true. But really, it's the stuff we never think to worry about that actually happens. Like exploding red pens or packets of fish food.

Despite Journee worrying that her idiotic brother had caused an unthinkable catastrophe, everything had turned out fine. Cave 6164 was a thing of beauty. The door was fixed, there were new lights surrounding the windows, and new cereal boxes were stacked neatly.

Journee stood at the front door with her parents and Miles by her side.

'Please, come in,' said Memory, blocking Panic in the nick of time. 'No rainbow lasers!' she said.

Panic shot just the one, into a nearby rock seat, which exploded instantly and coated the Blake family in dust.

'Sorry, awfully,' he sniffed. 'Slipped.'

Bill and Betty were asked to take their shoes

off, because rules were rules. Mr Blake grimaced as he tiptoed through slime and sludge. Betty didn't care one bit. She ran the slime through her fingers and said, 'We could sell this, we'd make a fortune.'

Inside the cave, candles twinkled. Mr Blake wiped the rocky seat with his handkerchief and chose to sit on the very edge so as not to get his trousers dirty. 'Nice pad you got here,' he said. 'Though it could do with a lick of paint. I'm Chief Sergeant now, did Journee mention that?' He reached into his jacket. 'I've got the newspaper clipping.'

Panic speed-read the article. 'Not as good as *Charlotte's Web*,' he scoffed, before being asked by Memory if he wouldn't mind bringing the starters. Panic shuffled across the cave and returned with fresh mud tea. 'That pot looks awfully familiar,' said Betty. 'She's only borrowing it,' Journee replied. 'And isn't that Miles' soccer ball?' asked Mr Blake.

'We're *family*,' said Journee.

'Speaking of which,' said Betty. 'You do know you white blobs are welcome to use our house whenever you like?'

'That would be wonderful, thank you,' said

Memory, giving Journee a knowing wink.

'Just be careful of the oven,' said Mr Blake. 'Takes a bit of getting used to.'

Memory nodded. 'Orange cake, anyone?' 'Hey, isn't that my plate?' asked Betty. 'Mum!' Journee said.

As Chime jumped onto Journee's lap, she stared at her family as they tried mud tea for the first time. Each sniffed the cup, screwed their noses up, and pretended to sip. Journee realised how silly she herself must have once looked.

Betty then took the floor. 'Memory, Panic, Chime, if I may say a few words. Firstly, thank you for allowing our daughter to become a part of your lives. I have never seen her so happy.'

Journee laid her head on Memory's shoulder and winked.

'Also,' Betty continued. 'Journee may not have told you, as she is not one to skite, but I am a businesswoman. So here's my idea. We tell the citizens of Millwater all about the secret people who live under the ground, and charge them lots of money. Before you know it, millions of tourists from all over the world will visit. You will be famous!'

'Beep off, jughead, toilet idea!'

'Thank you so much for the opportunity, it sounds wonderful,' Memory replied. 'But please be aware, you are the only Fuss Buckets who have ever seen us. Even meeting for dinner like this is very strange. If it's okay, we'd like to keep it that way.'

Soon, more food arrived and Mr Blake's eyes tripled in size when he smelt the dish. 'Hmm, yum, yum!' he said. 'A Chief Sergeant sure could get used to this kind of service.' He patted his belly and lifted the lid of the pot. 'What do you call this dish?'

'Popper casserole, sir!' said Panic.

'*Popper casserole?*' replied Mr Blake. 'What's that?'

'Cooked rat!' said Panic.

'HA!' scoffed Mr Blake, and ploughed into the dish like a starved seagull. 'You white blobs are hilarious!'

Memory turned to Journee, who did her very best to control her laughter. 'What about you, dear? Is your Fuss Bucket brother behaving himself?'

'Affirmative!' said Journee, laughing. 'I got my own room *and* a new phone.' She passed her old phone to the Underer. 'We can text each other. I can tell you when the coast is clear and Webster is in his cage.' Which triggered Journee's own memory.

There was something else she hadn't brought up, until now. 'The day we nearly lost you…I looked into the alarm and saw the tiny white things. I'm so sorry. Do you know what happened?'

'I know exactly what would have happened,' Memory replied in a soft voice. 'It's okay, dear. We are still here, and always will be. When will I see you again?'

'How about tomorrow?' Journee replied.

Memory nodded and held Journee tight in her arms. Journee looked through Cave 6164's window and across to the first step, which led to the secret door above.

What an adventure, she thought to herself. What an unbelievable gift.

Journee Blake would sleep very well tonight.

———

Important message:

The next time you see a shadow in the hallway, or hear a strange noise, look a little closer at your house alarm. You may be lucky enough to meet new friends. Perhaps they will bake you orange cake or show you a real live crocodile. Because when you're out they're in. You just have to find the secret door.

Also by Justin Christopher

Freakout Island

Five children are tricked into visiting a wonderfully magical island which becomes a hilarious and unexpected disaster. One small boy can save the day, if only he didn't have a gigantic bubble blowing out of his butt!

My Best Worst Year

A hilarious story about a boy who is promised a Gamebox V3 by his dad if he scores 20 wickets in cricket and 10 tries in rugby, but is foiled at every turn by the class bully.